The Diary of an Expectant Father:
Graham Peterson

Pete Sortwell

ISBN-13:978-1493714735
ISBN-10:1493714732

Dear Will,

I cannot wait to work with you on these books.

all the very best,

DEDICATION

To my mate, Lively.

Pete Sortwell

ACKNOWLEDGEMENTS

I wouldn't be able to get my work into your hands if it wasn't for the help of the team I employ, they work extremely hard to make sure what ends up on your kindle is a high quality. These people are:

Julie Lewthwaite, for her continued sterling work on turning my ramblings into something that I can charge money for.

http://www.mlwritingservices.co.uk/

Graham D. Lock, for the excellent covers he's provided me.

http://www.peopleperhour.com/people/graham-d/animator-graphic-designer-and-illu/177926

Finally, thanks to Jack Dean for his input on this when I was stuck. If you fancy a laugh, check out his YouTube Channel http://www.youtube.com/user/JaackMaate

I can't recommend each and every one of these people enough.

INTRODUCTION

I thought I'd keep a diary; I'm never, EVER going to show it to anyone, but I am going to bury it in the garden, sealed in a tightly wrapped plastic bag. I'm even going to put a photo in. Then one day, in three thousand years' time, it'll be read by the aliens that take over the world and they'll have an insight into what life was like for someone who was becoming a father for the first time. They'll probably make me an alien lord or something. If DNA technology is advanced enough, they could even bring me back to life. If you are an alien warlord or anything like that, there is a sample of my blood on the piece of cloth sellotaped to the back of this diary. Please only recreate me if you plan on giving me an easy life. I've also put a strand of my best friend Keith's hair in the back; if you need to anally probe anyone then please use this to bring him back instead. I've always suspected he'd be really into that, so you'd probably be doing him a favour.

Other than that I'm Graham Peterson, I'm twenty-eight, and it's the year 2012. If you're interested, England, where I live, is hosting the Olympic Games this year. That's a sporting event; or, more accurately, a series of sporting events. We're all completely underwhelmed. Most of London, our capital city, is closed off to make way for the people taking part, so normal people have to sit in traffic for far longer than they normally would.

Earth is a strange place at this time. You have to work all day for five days a week; we do this for most our lives and then we give up a couple of years before we die. I suppose you've moved on by now. Again, if you're able to recreate me into a world without work, then please do. I've a certificate in saving lives, so if any of your kind are planning on falling into swimming pools while wearing their pyjamas, I'm your man. For any other medical problems you're probably better off recreating someone else. David Attenborough might be a good bet.

Back to me, though … I'm an expectant father, I've not really got a clue what I'm doing and I thought writing this might give all your people in the future either an idea of how rubbish we were in the new millennium or go some way to helping me find a way out of my own worries. Either way it's a release for me and that's all I really care about.

So that's me. I'm a pretty normal guy who has found himself in a pretty normal situation. This is the story of the pregnancy and how I came to terms with being an expectant father.

JANUARY 2012

Wednesday January 26th 2012

5.30 p.m.

I'm not quite sure what to do with myself. I remember seeing a TV programme about how writing a diary is a release and can help people. That's all I can think to do as I don't think this is something that can be sorted by my normal solution to problems (a few pints in the pub with Keith); this is going to be long term.

Alison rang me this morning and said she needed to speak to me urgently. I reminded her we were on the phone and that it was a technical possibility to speak there and then, but she insisted that we do it in person. I hate it when people do that, more so as I still had six hours of work left and couldn't help but obsess about just what it could be. I'm meeting her in an hour, so going to shower and get ready.

10.00 p.m.

Well, it's happened … somehow I've managed to pass on my miserable seed to a woman who's kept it rather than rejected it, along with me, which is usually the case. Alison told me that she'd missed her period. I almost dropped my battered sausage. Why she waited until I was taking a bite to tell me, I don't know. I wasn't interested in carrying on eating after that, anyway. The shock was enough to put any man off a portion of Terry's excellent chips.

'How long have you known?' I asked.

'Well, I knew I'd missed it last week,' she told me.

After a few back and forth questions from me, which all seemingly had really obvious answers, we decided that we had to know for sure and that meant one thing: pregnancy test. We spent an hour in Boots looking at all the different types. You wouldn't believe how many different sorts of tests there are, digital, non-digital, double digital, it's crazy. Pink ones, blue ones, white ones, I don't know how anyone is supposed to make the choice based on anything other than price. All of them were ninety-nine point something per cent accurate. I mean if it's five quid and ninety-nine point nothing per cent accurate, it's going to be pretty good, what real difference does the point four or point five make? There can't be much difference in it. I noticed the most expensive one was almost twenty-five quid. Just as I was jamming it back on the shelf before Alison saw it and wanted it, because of the shiny box and wild claims of being ninety-nine point NINE per cent accurate, a couple of greasy looking women walked past me and snorted, telling one another that, 'You can get the same thing in Poundland, only for a quid.' All smug. I don't believe you can actually get pregnancy tests in Poundland so I didn't drag Alison over there, but we did manage to settle on a middle of the road test for eight pounds. It's ninety-nine point four per cent accurate.

'Sir, you can't go in there,' the security guard called after me as I followed Alison into the ladies. I didn't think it would matter if it was for official business, no funny stuff or looking at women weeing. He wouldn't have it, though, and followed me in to remove me physically.

Alison didn't want to do it without me there, although personally I didn't mind too much. I wasn't really too keen on seeing her do *that* anyway. But if I've learnt one thing tonight then it's that you don't disagree with a pregnant — or at that point a potentially pregnant — woman. She'd been drinking water all the way into town and by the time we managed to get rid of the security guard from the shopping centre, Alison was really angry and literally busting for a wee. She frantically looked around the centre for somewhere to go. I couldn't see any other outcome than her wetting herself and was working myself up thinking about how today wasn't going at all as I'd thought it would when I woke up this morning. 'In here,' Alison demanded, almost pulling my arm out the socket as she clambered into a photo booth.

I couldn't fit into the booth, so I had to stand with my head poking through the curtain while Alison hiked up her skirt, pulled her pants down and let the river flow, as it were. I was so busy concentrating on the stick to see if it lit up or beeped or whatever it was we were going to get for our eight quid that I didn't notice the river of urine that was pouring out the booth onto the floor, via my shoes. As quick as she'd started

Alison finished and did the most inconsiderate thing I've ever known her to do: she flicked the piss stick and sprayed the only part of my body that was in the photo booth – my face. I got pregnant piss in my eyes, mouth and nose. I'd been given a golden face shower. I'm sure there are some weirdos out there that would have paid money to have a similar thing happen to them. I am not one of them.

It was as I stepped backwards that I noticed the river, well, I say noticed … I mean slipped in. I had piss on my face and piss on my shoes. Then Alison said that we needed to wait five minutes for the test to dry. 'It'll probably be done in two,' I said wiping most of what had been on the stick off my face as we headed away from the mess we'd made as quickly as we could.

It wasn't a big celebration when the line stayed blue and the instructions told us that she was pregnant. If I'm honest, Diary, for one of the most important moments of my adult life, I was angry about having been covered in piss. So angry that all I could really think of was not that there would be a little bundle of joy in my life soon, but that I would be able to get home and have a regular shower designed for normal people soon. Alison just looked shocked. Then I don't suppose a girl grows into a woman thinking that she'll find out she's to be a mother after defacing a Kodak photo booth.

I walked Alison to the taxi rank, promised I'd call her tomorrow and came home to empty a bottle of Radox into my eyes.

I'm not sure how I feel really. Other than dirty, that is. I'll reassess in the morning.

1.00 a.m.

I've just woken up in a cold sweat. This is massive. How will I cope? What will I do? Can I afford it? How am I going to tell my parents? Life is going to change drastically in nine months.

Too many questions.

Thursday January 27th 2012

I hardly slept a wink after I'd woken up in a sweat. All I could think about was how there are so many ways in which I can screw this up. Alison seems so in control and with it. Well, she didn't sound scared on the phone, anyway, far from it. She sounded excited. We've only been together a few weeks. I hope I've not been trapped in a honey trap or whatever they call it these days. I've read about women like that in the paper. They get men into bed, get pregnant, and then latch onto them for life, like an evil stick insect.

I like Alison, I like her a lot. I mean I have to, she's the only woman who hasn't dumped me after three or four dates. Except for the incident with the piss yesterday, but I've decided to chalk that one down to experience and never again go anywhere near a photo booth while a woman, mine or anyone else's, is taking a pregnancy test in there. It's my own fault; I should have seen the danger in that situation. I was like a child wandering out into the road, no sense of the impending doom that awaited me. She's not a bad person, either. Anyone who looks after old people for a living can't be a bad person, She's also a qualified nurse, it's always good to have a nurse about the place.

Today dragged, I couldn't concentrate on the job in hand. Jane, my boss, started me off on the grill, which meant I had to cook all the bacon and have it ready for when the workers came in between seven and nine, then keep it going but also make sure that there was a supply of cheese on toast, too. It takes skill and timing to get it right when one is feeling OK with the world, and today I wasn't, which meant some of the workers got bacon that had only been cooked on one side, and the queue for cheese on toast was huge.

If the workers lean over the counter a bit they can see who's working the grill and tend to shout over 'Hurry the fuck up' if the cheese on toast isn't coming quick enough. I've told Jane that we need more grills in order to get the most popular item cooked and served quicker, but she's not made it happen. It's tense work and today I just couldn't do it. Once I'd dropped a tray of the stuff in front of the eyes of the very people waiting for it, Jane realised that if she wanted to get through the day without having to deal with endless complaints forms (which dictate our weekly bonus) it was time to move me to something less important.

That job was loading and unloading the dishwasher, which is the worst job in the kitchen and normally considered punishment. On the plus side, Boris was delighted to come off dishwasher duty and stop being punished for drinking the cooking wine three weeks ago. I think three weeks' washing up isn't punishment enough for drinking at work, but apparently dropping cheese on toast is worse than that. Still, I didn't have to deal with people shouting, or any scalding hot cheese that not only burns when it comes into contact with skin, but also sticks to it.

It's fair to say that today wasn't good. I spent the remainder of the shift loading and unloading the dishwasher. It was nice to have such a simplistic job, actually, as it allowed my mind to wander, but not too much. I went through the fears I had one by one and tried to think about them in a logical way. Here is my list of fears:

That I'll be a terrible father.

That the baby won't like me.

That I'll somehow screw up the kid so it ends up being a mass murderer or something.

That if the above happens, *The Sun* will do an investigation into the killer's family and expose me as a loser.

That Alison will run off with the baby and I'll be one of those fathers that doesn't get to see his kid until he dresses up like Batman and climbs something tall.

That I won't be able to afford a baby.

That it'll grow up and be like me.

That the baby will have a disability and be reliant on me for life.

That the baby will have ADHD and be an absolute nightmare.

That my nights will become even more sleepless.

When I've listed it like, that I'm glad I only went through them one at a time as that is a terrifying list to see all in one go.

Here is my rationale:

You might be, but everyone learns and there are classes on being a good father and loads of books you can read, doing this might just upgrade you from 'terrible' to 'mildly pathetic'.

Babies don't dislike people, they don't know how to. I can manipulate it into liking me.

See point 1, but also research on the Internet 'how to make sure your child isn't a killer'.

See points 1 and 3.

I'll have to ask Alison to marry me, she'll always be traceable then as she'll have my name.

I've thought more and more about this and if I marry Alison, then we'll live together and we'll have more money. Failing that, we could both give up work; I read all the time in the paper that people who don't work have more money than people who do. Failing that, I could stop spending all my money on myself. So there are options.

Of course it might. OR it might grow up and be like Alison. If we raise it like Alison then everything will be alright. Either that or I completely change my life around. I think it would be easier to raise it like Alison.

This is a natural fear all parents have, and most babies don't have disabilities or the human race wouldn't survive.

That'll be payback for me being a nightmare.

Ear plugs are cheap and Alison will be off work anyway, so she'll be happy to get up and look after the little one.

Just an extra: this is all months away. I don't need to worry so much. Nine months takes ages to pass.

Not a complete saviour of a list, but it certainly got me through the day at the dishwasher.

Alison has been on the phone this evening asking when we are going to make the news public. By 'public' she means telling her mum and then putting it on Facebook. I suggested we wait at least until we've been to the doctor's before we spoke to her parents, Alison wasn't so sure. Well, I say wasn't sure, she'd already told her mum, who in turn has told her dad. I think she did it last night as soon as she got home. I've not even met either of her parents yet. I suppose I'll have to at some point now.

I think I'll start another 'fears' list.

Friday January 28th 2012

Seeing as I'm writing a diary, I might as well tell you how it all started with Alison. Just in case all you alien warlords are interested in human relations.

I was out on my work's Christmas meal; we went for Mexican food, which I still think was chosen on purpose because everyone knew that I didn't actually like Mexican food. It wasn't at all Christmassy. Thankfully I've left the Bus Company now and have a new job in the local department store's staff kitchen. It's a bit of a better job and there's free food, so it's not terrible.

Anyway, back to the Christmas night out. After I'd been coaxed into eating some vile mince that was so spicy it tasted like pen ink, Joey, the popular confident manager, convinced me that a tequila would 'cleanse my palate' – which was a complete lie. That was like pouring petrol into my mouth, which on top of the taste of pen ink caused me to be sick, which luckily went mostly under the table. I did feel the effect of the tequila, though, and it was good. Within a few minutes I didn't care about embarrassing myself by being sick. So, on Joey's advice I had a couple more and joined in with the dancing. I didn't even care that everyone I worked with was pointing, laughing and filming me; I was enjoying myself. The evening went on and we ended up in a club. That was where I met Alison.

She was dancing on her own, but she explained that she had been with friends and definitely isn't the type of loser that goes clubbing on her own. In a way I'm glad that my work colleagues had their phone cameras pointed at me all night in the hope of catching something they could put on Facebook, as they caught the first kiss between me and Alison, the first dance, the first fumble outside the club, it's all there on Facebook ready for when I get old and want to look back on my life. I knew they were doing it to take the piss, but this time the joke was on them because Alison was at my house the next morning.

I wasn't a virgin before I met her, but I wasn't exactly well versed in sex … and I still wasn't, as I couldn't really remember if we'd done 'it' or not. It's not the sort of thing that you should really ask the person you wake up next to, so I was more than pleased when Alison asked *me* if we'd had sex. It was the first thing she said, actually. When I replied with a blank look on my face, she dug her hands under the covers for a minute, had a shufty round then confirmed that she thought we had. I don't even want to know what it was she was doing, but I was glad that I could go into work and tell everyone that I'd definitely done 'it' and declare the graffiti on the wall invalid.

I didn't tell anyone in the end. As it turns out, I left the bus company that day. By which I mean I never returned. I spent the day with Alison and once we got talking I told her about how much I hated working there. I told her how everyone took the piss and treated me like something they found at the back of a bus after a shift. It was Alison that suggested I look for another job, which was something I'd thought about myself but had never really got round to. I suppose I was scared. I mean, what if I left and found a job at somewhere more terrible? What if they wanted me to work longer hours than I was comfortable with? With Alison, though, I had someone to talk my fears through with and she empowered me to look into it. That's what she's like, she makes things happen, and within two days I'd secured a new job with a much smaller team in a much nicer company. That's almost three months ago now and most days I'm happy there. It's all thanks to Alison. Jane is no summer breeze or anything, but even her little paddies are nothing compared to what I put up with at the bus company.

Today was a better day at work, I managed to get off punishment dishwasher duty and Boris was put back on it for dropping five pies in separate incidents yesterday after Jane put him on serving up. It was nice to be back on the deep fat fryer. I like it there as I get to have a break while watching whatever it is that I've just chucked in. it just floats to the top when it's ready. There's no variant. Whenever something is cooked in a deep fat fryer, it floats to show it's done, so there's no watching the clock or turning it over, I just stand there until I see it. It's probably my favourite job, except on Fridays when it's fish and chip day, then it's a nightmare as chef has us batter the fish ourselves and it's always really messy. I try to get put on punishment duty late on a Thursday and let Boris deal with cleaning all the batter up.

Friday is also the day that we have to clean the fat out the fryers and that's the worst job in the kitchen, hands down. It really is vile. It's all white and hard by the time it's cooled. Anytime I can manipulate the situation for Boris to clean it, I will. It might sound horrible, Diary, but it's the way it is and I'm fairly sure Boris doesn't mind. Anyway, it's his own fault for losing his driving licence for drink-driving. He was a taxi driver before he worked here. So really he should be doing the horrible jobs. Maybe next time he has a licence he'll look after it more carefully. He'll probably thank me for it one day.

I didn't do much at all this evening except try and lose myself in my writing, although it's just my luck that I was writing about the exact issue I was trying to escape.

I wonder if this is something that happens in your time or place? I doubt it, I suppose, being as advanced as you are, you don't concern yourself with fear or anything like that.

Monday January 30th 2012

On the way home from work I had a moment of panic as I was walking through town and ran into Boots to buy the ninety-nine point nine per cent accurate pregnancy test. I'll give it to Alison when I see her tomorrow. I hope it shows negative, I don't think I can handle being a father.

I texted Alison tonight; she hasn't been to work today, she's taken the week off sick. I wish I could just take the week off and get paid for it.

Tuesday January 31st 2012

Alison was less than enthusiastic about the double digital test I presented her with when I got round there this evening. Turns out she'd bought three of them herself and didn't have any money left because of it. Neither did I, as I don't get paid till the end of the week and I'd spent the last of my money on the test. Her parents were out so I didn't meet them, thank God.

I thought I'd get dinner at Alison's, but I didn't want to tell her I had no money and when she said they'd already had theirs I felt bad asking. When we got back to mine I grabbed some tuna, pasta and mayonnaise, although I didn't have any mayo so I used salad cream instead. Alison was hungry again so I gave her some.

She did nothing but complain about the dinner I lovingly prepared for her, demanding I wash all the salad cream off as she couldn't eat it whilst pregnant. I, of course, did as requested then had to listen to her moan about how dinner didn't taste of anything.

Alison said she couldn't walk back home as she felt sick. I suspect she was lying.

FEBRUARY 2012

Friday February 3rd 2012

Pay day today, so I ordered a book from Amazon: *Pregnancy For Men, Getting Through The First Nine Months.* Hopefully it'll help me.

I asked Alison if she'd booked the doctor's appointment yet; she said she hadn't, but is going to today. I think she's putting it off. She's staying at her house tonight so I'll get to stretch out in bed.

Whoever named it 'morning' sickness is a liar. Alison is sick mainly during the afternoon, and then in the evening feels like she is going to be, but isn't. She keeps texting me to let me know she's feeling bad. I've no idea what I'm supposed to say to her back.

Saturday February 4th 2012

I spent the morning walking to Morrisons and back. I thought if I walked I'd save a bit of money, although walking all the way home carrying a week's shopping almost finished me off. It's all uphill. I'm not sure what I was thinking about.

I've never thought about not spending all my money every week, but I suppose I'd better start. To make sure I saved it I popped into the bank before heading home and changed up the twenty quid into one penny and two pence pieces. I've put them all in my huge Coke bottle along with the buttons and foreign money I keep in there.

This afternoon I was supposed to meet Alison, but she cancelled as she was feeling ill. I think she might be going off me. I've not seen her much at all since I made her dinner.

I text her three or four times an hour just to make sure she knows I'm still interested.

Sunday February 5th 2012

Alison turned up at my house at 1 a.m. this morning. Drunk. She kept repeating that she wasn't ready to be a mother. Then she was sick on my sofa before passing out. In the sick.

I had to clean up while she lolled about in the sick, spreading it over all the places I'd just cleaned. I'm quite good at cleaning up sick. It's a better job than cleaning the deep fat fryer, and on par with cleaning out the blocked drain of the dishwasher after Boris chucks the plates he hasn't rinsed in there.

I stayed up until 6 a.m. making sure that she wasn't sick again. I checked YouTube and made sure her airways were open. I wouldn't want the baby to lose any oxygen. I dropped off in the chair in the end. I woke around nine to hear Alison finishing emptying her stomach in my toilet. It was time for tears at the breakfast table then, after I'd made her a cup of tea.

'I'm just scared, Graham,' she explained. And it was time for me to do something that I've never done before: comfort someone who needed it. I normally shy away from that sort of thing, shrink behind whoever else is in the vicinity. You can't really do that in front of the only person in the room, though. Especially when you are the one that is the cause of the problem.

We ended up having a pretty frank discussion. We both talked about the fears we had. I didn't share all my list with her as when I started to say some of it, it sounded really selfish, which doesn't make it less valid, but it *is* selfish nevertheless. Alison didn't hold back in any way, though. Most of her fears were about me. What if I ran off, what If I was a terrible father (which I did agree with and said so). Then she said something that scared me.

'What if it screams and I can't handle it and I kill it?' she wept, looking up at me with smudged makeup and crusty sick round her mouth.

I hugged her. Christ, I actually hugged her. Could this mean I love her? I would never normally hug someone that looked like that after they'd just said something like that.

'You won't kill it, darling,' was about all I could say.

I hope that book hurries up and gets here, then I'll have all the answers to questions like this.

'But what If I do? I'll get arrested,' Alison said, answering her own question. I managed to divert the conversation there by giving her a glass of water that made her run to the toilet as soon as she swallowed a mouthful.

She also admitted that she's still not contacted the doctor as she doesn't want it to become real. I managed to persuade her it was the best thing to do and she's agreed to do it this week.

We spent the rest of the day trying to get food to stay inside Alison. We finally managed it with some chicken soup. And although there was little more I could do than hold her hair, I think Alison appreciated that I was there.

I didn't talk to her about getting drunk in this state. She did keep saying, over and over again, that she'd never drink again so I don't think I'll need to. I took her home before the news as it's a work day tomorrow and I didn't fancy having to take her before I went there. I was also tired and wanted to sleep tonight. I'd had enough of talking, to be honest. I needed sleep.

11.45 p.m.

I couldn't sleep when I got home, so I read my book.

I've read that up to twelve weeks there is a higher risk of losing the baby. Apparently if there is a history of miscarriages in the family, there is more chance of it happening. Also, there is a chance that the baby could have Down's syndrome. I had to Google this, as I thought that was the thing that happened when you went diving and came up too quick. It's not though, that's called 'bends'. Down's is a different thing entirely. I've met a few people with Down's syndrome in the past and they all seemed nice enough. There was a lad at school called David and he loved life. I suppose the physical side of things and the learning problems that come with it are pretty debilitating. It's for life, too. Everywhere on the Internet is suggesting that it would be a good idea to do the test that they can do for it. This needs to be done at the twelve week scan

It's strange the reason everyone is suggesting that the test is done at that point is so that terminations can still be carried out. I've been thinking about this and I think it's pretty unfair to terminate someone's life, however many weeks away they may be from entering this world on the account that they might have Down's syndrome. I'm not comfortable with doing something like that.

I suppose that's one of the downsides to modern science. Where will it end, though? A missing finger – terminated; a funny looking eye – terminated. I suppose for some really horrible things, like having no arms or legs, it is something to think about ... but even that, I've seen a guy on the Internet who hasn't got any and he seems really happy, in fact, he does talks about it and goes swimming. He's got a little bit of a foot on one side of his torso and makes extra use of that. It's pretty amazing, really. In the world of 'get rid of the wrong', though, this chap wouldn't be around to go and talk at all sorts of colleges and summits about how happiness is an inside job.

I doubt anyone reading this in the future will have to make such decisions; I suspect that the same science that makes it possible now for people to rid themselves of problems, will have developed to be able to fix any problems before the birth.

I can't think about it anymore.

Monday February 6th 2012

I texted Alison:

Morning Babe, I hope you're feeling better today. Don't worry about what you said yesterday, I'm great at judging the murderers on the news when they do press conferences. No way you're like them weirdos. X

She replied to say she's booked the doctor's appointment for tomorrow at ten. I've told Jane I've got to go for myself. I'm not going to tell her about the baby until I absolutely have to, you hear such horror stories about people getting sacked for having kids.

Tuesday February 7th 2012

I took Alison to see the doctor this morning. We were in there an hour and a half; mind you, only twenty-five minutes of that was actually time spent in front of a medical professional. The rest of the time we were just sitting in the waiting room collecting diseases off all the other people waiting.

We went in and the doctor took a blood sample off Alison and gave her abdomen the once-over with a machine that was hooked up to a microphone. We could hear the baby's heart beating through the belly. It's a moment I'll never forget. It sounded really strong, like whoever it is in there had been running. I suppose it's hard work making yourself into a person out of nothing, I'd be shagged out, too.

The blood test results will be with us tomorrow, the urine test they ran was also positive. I noticed that it was just one of the mid-range tests we'd seen for sale in Boots, but just in a plain box rather than a full colour one with all the adverts and claims of ninety-nine point four per cent accuracy.

The midwife was nice and put Alison at ease. We left in almost no doubt that we're going to be parents. She is going to ring us tomorrow and tell us about the process.

She did say that she'd book us in for the ultrasounds, though. I asked when we could find out if it was a boy or a girl. 'Just twenty weeks, love. Not long if you're as far along as you think,' she replied.

She's right – if Alison's last period was over two months ago, we've only got a few weeks and then we're at the scan.

The midwife did say we should think about not telling people until the twelve-week point. I looked at Alison and raised an eyebrow at that point. The midwife understood what was happening. I was grassing Alison up to the midwife, that's what was happening.

Alison 'accidentally' spilt hot coffee over me in the cafe after. My white trainers are now stained.

I didn't bother going back into work today. I rang Jane and said that I had been sent to the hospital for a test and there was a wait. She said it was OK this time, but not to make it a regular thing. I promised not to.

After Alison went to bed, I got on the Internet and started looking at Down's syndrome information. I couldn't find any famous people that had it, but there have been some great achievers.

Wednesday February 8th 2012

The midwife called Alison at around ten; Alison, in turn, called me straight away. Jane said I could take the call, but only because I had already answered it. Boris had a celebratory drink of the cooking wine when I told him the news. He's the only person I've told and he's promised he won't tell anyone.

I've been thinking about Down's syndrome. Boris, who called it mongaloydolia said that it's very common in Russia, due to all the metal in the water, put there by the KGB to keep the numbers of people low. He seems convinced that if a baby is named 'Boris' as soon as the parents find out they're pregnant then it won't occur. He really is an idiot.

Alison wants to tell everyone now, but I've insisted we hold off until I've told my parents.

I spent the rest of the day checking her Facebook to make sure she didn't announce it. She hasn't done as yet.

11.00 p.m.

I can't sleep. In nine months I'm going to be a father. I work in a kitchen. This is not a good combination.

11.45 p.m.

I keep thinking about having to make a decision if the baby has Down's syndrome. Alison still doesn't know I have this worry, she's not mentioned it either. I keep thinking about David running about on the football pitch and the time he laughed until he had to be helped to get up. I don't want to have to think about getting rid of David or his little counterpart.

Thursday February 9th 2012

Keith phoned this evening. He wants to go for a drink tomorrow night after work. I suppose I better go or he'll think something is up and start turning up at my house all the time like he did last time he assumed I'd harmed myself.

I don't really want to have to make the decision re the Down's syndrome test. I've read there can be some problems with the actual test, which is crazy. How can they have a test that can cause more harm than good? It's completely ridiculous. I suppose it's the same as some of the antidepressants out there that actually have suicide ideation as side effects. I kid you not.

I've decided I'm not going to bring up the conversation with Alison about Down's syndrome. I'm not sure what her views are on it. I don't want to start a row, I'm still not sure what my own views are. It just feels wrong to get rid of someone just because they have a disability that might make things a bit difficult for us. I'll see if she brings it up.

I think I'll speak to Keith about it.

Friday February 10th 2012

I went out with Keith tonight. I didn't tell Alison that's why I wanted her to go home, but I needed to run things past him. He was shocked when I told him. Then he asked if I was winding him up. He could tell by the look on my face that I wasn't, though.

'Keeping it, then?' was Keith's first question.

'Of course I'm fucking keeping it!' I told him. 'I wouldn't be telling you about it if we were planning on terminating it,' I added, using the terminology I learnt from my book.

'Hard work, there, mate,' he said.

'I know. Think it could be pretty cool, though. You could be Godfather if you like?' I asked.

'I'm not Christian, though,' Keith said seriously.

'You don't need to be. I don't even think we do,' I informed him.

'Oh, OK. Yeah, I'll do it. What you having, a girl or a boy?'

'They don't tell you until you're twenty weeks gone.'

'Interesting stuff,' Keith confirmed, taking a sup of his shandy.

I wanted to ask Keith about the Down's syndrome thing but I got nervous. I didn't want him to think I was being an arse. Some people get funny about things like that and any questions raised against the government advice that is rolled out at GP's surgeries and hospitals is considered wrong; it's all accepted as fact without any sort of scrutiny at all. Keith is one of those people. I'm not. I hate the way we are force-fed lies by the people that are supposed to be our trusted servants. Anyway, I didn't tell Keith. It's something I need to sort out in my own head.

That was all he had to say about things, really; he had a few more silly questions throughout the evening, but mainly we just played *Call of Duty* and talked about that.

It was nice to be out the house, though, and a bit of escapism in a virtual killing game did the trick nicely.

Saturday February 11th 2012

I rang my parents tonight. Mum answered. Dad was outside fixing his shed. God knows what it was he was fixing, as every time I go round he tells me how wonderful it is and that being able to build your own shed is what makes a man.

I invited myself round to dinner tomorrow and told Mum I would be bringing a woman with me. Once she'd stopped screaming with excitement, the questions started. 'What does she like to eat? What doesn't she like? Shall we go out? Shall we get a takeaway? Oh, I better tell your dad to change out of his overalls to eat. What time are you coming? Is it tea, dinner or supper where she comes from? Shall we sit in the kitchen, lounge or dining room?' My answer to all of these was, 'You decide, Mum. She's nice; don't worry.'

I texted Alison and told her, then got asked a similar amount of questions. 'What shall I wear? Are we eating in or out? Do I need to bring anything? They're not doing sprouts, are they? Did you tell them I'm pregnant?'

The last question stopped me repeating, 'Don't worry.' I didn't, but I'm going to have to tell them tomorrow – it's why we're going round.

I spent the rest of the evening playing out different scenarios in my head. There was: they take it well, jumping for joy and telling me they're proud of me; they reject Alison and the unborn; one of them is happy and the other one goes quiet. Then reverse that one: we are asked to leave; we are asked to move in to save money; they suggest a meeting between the two families to talk out the crisis; they suggest a meeting between the two families to 'get to know each other better'. All this played out in great detail well into the early hours, when I decided to get up and write this.

Sunday February 12th 2012

We arrived at my parents' house early this afternoon. This caused Mother to flap, as Dad hadn't found his way in from the shed yet and she still had her apron on. Honestly, I think she'd done nothing but obsess about making the perfect dinner since I put the phone down yesterday.

I had to stand in the way of Mum so she wouldn't keep hugging Alison; she kept looking around me, though, and trying to get close for the hug. In the end, Dad distracted me by almost falling through the back door. Bless him, he'd been trying to play it cool but as soon as he heard my mother's excitement he caught the bug and must have sprinted in from the shed.

'Oh, you're here!' He announced feigning surprise and clambering over Mum, offering his hand to Alison.

Once the excitement had died down and everyone was wearing what my mother thought they should be, we sat down to eat. The roast lamb Mum had done smelled lovely. Unfortunately it didn't smell that lovely to Alison and she had to excuse herself. Quickly.

A knowing look went from Dad to Mum and back again, once she'd cottoned on to what he was trying to say. I just nodded. I think it was a bit of a jokey look that my father gave my mother, but all too quickly they realised that they'd got something right. Then silence. We've never spoken about them being grandparents before, it's never seemed likely as I've never been with anyone long enough for it to be a consideration.

When Alison returned we all started to make small talk, like we didn't want to let Alison in on it. She must have sensed something had happened by the way both my parents were now looking at the top of the curtain rail. She just looked at me and smiled then shrugged.

'Are you happy?' Mum asked her, not being able to avoid the situation any longer.

'I think we are,' Alison said, reaching out for my hand and holding it on top of the table. She looked into my eyes and regardless of the fact she'd just chucked up I felt something. Just an emotional stirring. Maybe it's the flutter of love, I don't know. I do know the moment was broken by Mum going 'Aww,' for a little longer than was necessary. I actually think she just wanted us to get on and eat the lamb she'd spent all morning cooking.

Later on, when we'd finished off the homemade pavlova, we sat and talked. The bottom line of the conversation was, 'We haven't got loads of money, but we'll help where we can;' 'We're pleased for you;' and, 'When can we meet your parents, Alison?'

Then, as Dad was showing me the new electricity cable he'd rigged up in the shed, he whispered to me that I should probably ask Alison to marry me. He didn't say it in a way that I could argue with or even comment on as he started handing me stuff that needed loading into the back of the shed.

I asked my mum about Down's when Alison was distracted by my dad's new huge drill. 'You remember David, don't you?' she said. I told her I'd been thinking about him a lot lately. We went to school together and he was pretty clever, he learnt with the rest of us and even did better in his exams than some of the other students. Fair enough, those others normally spent most of their time standing outside lessons waiting to be allowed back in. David, was always on time for school and was happy nearly all the time, the only time I ever saw him angry was when his bag was thrown into the road on the way to swimming and got run over. His reaction to the kid who did it ensured no one ever took the Mickey out of him again though, he went WILD and good on him for doing so.

Swimming was the only sport he was allowed to do; as he had a hole in the heart the school didn't want to be responsible for him having a heart attack during a game of football. It didn't stop him playing it every lunchtime though, he used to run himself ragged and wasn't interested in the danger the grown ups told him he was putting himself in. He was just a normal kid, really, if anything he was more energetic than the rest of us.

It's worrying me that Alison might want to get rid of a child that had this syndrome. I mean, I can't believe as a society we do that, I know in the deep Amazon they drown children that have disabilities when they're born, which I can kind of understand as they are primitive tribes, but we are a civilised society. I mean, if we're prepared to do that to someone, where does it stop? Killing off left-handed babies because we don't like the way they hold a pen? It's not something I wish to be a part of. Really, I should start a campaign or something. Although there's probably not much point, as I'm sure there are far more important people in the world than me who I'm sure have discussed this issue.

I know in China there is a big market for drugs that are supposed to make it more likely a woman will have a baby boy. There, you're only allowed a couple of kids so if you want your name to live on there aren't that many chances to get it right. I don't mean 'right' in everyone's eyes, I'm not going to mind what we have as long as it's happy, I mean 'right' in the eyes of the Chinese parents. I'm not sure what all the fuss is about in keeping the name going, there are loads of Petersons, and loads of every other name in the world, so it's just a big fuss about nothing, I suppose. Unless it's about bloodlines, but that doesn't make sense as girls carry them on too.

I'm not sure how Alison feels about all this so I'm not going to say anything to her, I hope she's not got a 'get rid of them' attitude, if she has I'm not sure how I'll deal with it.

Overall the day went well. Alison wasn't scared of my parents and we got out without agreeing to move closer or anything like that.

I'm not going to think too much about what Dad said about marriage. It's old fashioned these days, I think.

Monday February 13th 2012

Alison hasn't been to work for ages. She says her back hurts after a day on the wards. I thought a nurse would be more committed and at least have some contacts in the maternity section that would help her deal with pregnancy better, but she says she doesn't really know anyone as they all keep themselves to themselves and have cliques which nurses that have recently transferred from other hospitals have to work to get into. It sounds rubbish. She says I shouldn't worry about her not being there, as she can't be sacked for being pregnant, it's one of the few perks there is of working for a government run organisation.

I had to go in, though. It was a typical Monday. Boris told me he'd had a barbecue at the weekend. It smelled like he'd eaten alcoholic barbecue sauce. I didn't think to ask him at the time where or why he was having a barbecue in February. I suppose he was either lying or is really weird.

Jane was in a strop today; Boris kept dropping things. In the end she sent him off to steady his nerves with the cooking wine. It didn't cheer her up when he came back with two empty bottles, though; I think she'd intended to have a glass as well. You've got to admire his gall, mind.

This evening we just watched TV and ate food that didn't taste of anything. Alison has given me an extensive list of things that she can't eat. I did mushrooms on toast tonight. It was crying out for an egg on top, but Alison can't eat them so I'll have to continue stuffing my face at work and eating her food in the evening.

Tuesday February 14th 2012

It was Valentine's day today and I forgot to get Alison a card. Even worse, she remembered and gave one to me before I went to work. I lied and said I'd left hers at work so that I could give her it, along with some flowers, tonight. I made out she'd ruined her own surprise, but I actually forgot the biggest day of the year for lovers. I've only ever had a girlfriend once before on Valentine's day and that was when I was nine. She bought me a huge card that I ended up having to carry around school for the rest of the day.

I'm sure if I hadn't had the recent news I'd have been thinking about little other than how to make sure Alison knew how much I appreciated her being in my life.

I took her out this evening, once I'd given her the flowers and the card – which she loved. The film we went to watch was OK; it was called *Valentine's Day* and was a bit weepy. I could hear Alison sobbing through the sad bits. I didn't look at her, though, I didn't want her to see how wide I was holding my eyes open. I squeezed her hand a little, just to let her know I was there for her.

We had far too many sweets in the cinema; I knew I shouldn't have topped up with popcorn and ice cream. I wanted Alison to know that I knew how to treat a girl, though.

We were both sick when we got home, Alison through 'morning' sickness. Me, I was sick just through intake. I'm not sure I've had as much sugar since I was a child and ate all my Christmas selection box before dinner.

Still, I got to spend the evening with the woman in my life, even if we did pass out from a sugar crash.

Wednesday February 15th 2012

I've consulted my book and Alison shouldn't be eating all the sugar we did yesterday. It isn't good for baby and Alison could end up being diabetic, so it seems that I've put my girlfriend and my unborn at risk for the sake of a Valentine's present.

When I got home tonight Alison was still in her dressing gown. She hasn't done anything today. I asked if she was still feeling sick, and she told me that it was worse today. I decided not to tell her about the sugar. I'll tell her when she has forgotten about my poisoning attempt yesterday.

Saturday February 18th 2012

Tonight we went to a play Alison insisted she wanted to see. I wasn't really interested in seeing this or any other play, particularly, but I was interested in seeing Alison, as I haven't seen her for a couple of days. The play itself wasn't bad, but I couldn't help but judge the woman playing the queen; she was flouncing about on the stage, waffling on about how she felt about the kitchen hand and how it wouldn't be right for her to ravage him. When she did get round to taking all his clothes off, she discovered the kitchen hand wasn't a he, but a she. Then it was double taboo time: she wanted to have the poor girl beheaded for treason, then at the last minute realised she couldn't, as she loved her, and that it was all her fault for having such sexist laws of the land that it meant women could only work in the garden or on the market. That was about it. It was mainly just a monologue from the queen and her angst about being an arse, which she was. She needed to accept that.

I can't remember the last time I went to the theatre. I think it must have been when I was at school and they took us to see Johnny Ball. Tonight was more enjoyable than that and not just because the company I was in wasn't shoving popcorn down my shirt.

Alison and I walked home; it was a nice evening for February.

We didn't get too heavy into conversation about our fears of what is going to happen and how things are going to be. It was just nice to get out and have a normal evening. We're still getting to know each other, really. With all that's gone on in the short time we've known each other, I forget sometimes that I've only known Alison a couple of months. The more I get to know her, though, the more I like her.

Sunday February 19th 2012

Alison is convinced that she can feel something moving inside her. I'm not so sure, though; it's only been a few weeks. I certainly couldn't feel anything when I put my hand there. I double checked.

We looked at the BBC website as they have pictures on there. The baby looks like a cross between a dinosaur and a manatee. It's not a pretty sight at this stage. I started to get a bit competitive about things and started to actively prove Alison wrong about feeling the baby. It turns out I was right, we won't start feeling anything until at least weeks sixteen or seventeen. I didn't feel like I'd won, though. Alison just became upset and went to lie down.

I stayed up looking at the BBC site some more. There is absolutely loads of information on there. It's all in week by week sections. It's amazing what the human body – well, two human bodies – can produce between them. The baby grows from nothing into something baby-shaped, really tiny, but nevertheless, baby-shaped in less than twelve weeks. The nature side of things really is miraculous.

I haven't paid my TV licence in years. I might start to after I've found one thing that's worth looking at on a BBC site/channel. They've done really well.

It was midnight when I'd finished going through all the weeks.

I might take tomorrow off; I don't know if I can be bothered listening to whatever Boris did at the weekend.

Saturday February 25th 2012

Alison dragged me into town today, she wanted to buy her own microphone machine to listen to her belly. I've learnt two things today: 1) that the machines are called doppler machines and 2) no one who works in electrical shops knows they are called this. It took visits to Argos, Comet, PC World (Alison's idea) and finally Mothercare to find one. Still, she got one in the end, then spent almost as much on the cream that comes with it.

Alison spent the rest of the day listening to her belly through the machine. It sounds like a 1980s scanner that you're trying to listen to the police on. There's far too much crackling and not enough action. The baby actually moves about, too, which doesn't help. I don't suppose being prodded with something through the wall is an enjoyable experience though. I'd move away.

While I was catching up on my emails, I could hear Alison on the phone to her mother, the machine crackling away. I think she went through her phone book ringing everyone she knows. I didn't see her again until much later. She was happy, though; she's started the bonding process.

I've listened a few times and it's good to hear that the heart is still beating, but I don't feel the need to keep checking.

MARCH 2012

Saturday March 10th 2012

I've not written much for a while as it's mainly been a case of holding back Alison's hair and her continuing to staying at mine. I still don't know if she's actually moved in or not. She hasn't left for almost a month now. Well, she's left the flat, but only to go to the doctor's or the health food shop, and most of the time I do that for her. I don't know how to confirm the situation. It seems rude just to ask, but surely we need to be clear as to what the situation is. She seems quite happy being here. I could do with my own space a bit, though.

Maybe I should suggest she pops back to hers and then hide when she gets back. Or I could find an illness on the Internet that is bad for pregnant woman and then pretend I have it, then she'll have to go home.

It's not that I'm heartless or anything, I just want ... no, *need* ... time for me. We've not even been together long enough to live together. I'm going to stop thinking about it because all I do is worry that we're not ready to have a baby.

Mum and Dad have popped round a couple of times and have brought special sleeping pillows for Alison. Mum also had some potions that worked for her when she had gas and indigestion. I'm glad she did, as the burps Alison has been doing have been less than ladylike to say the least. She won't need the pillows for a while yet, but from what I've read in my book and on the BBC site, come the months when the bump really starts coming out, she'll be really uncomfortable in the night. I'll probably have to get the spare room set up for me. I'll be a gentleman and let her stay in the big bed.

Got to go – I can hear Alison throwing up. It's hair-holding time. I'm sure once we've finished doing that, we'll be checking what the doppler machine is saying.

9.00 p.m.

Alison spoke to me today about the Down's thing. It wasn't the, 'Sit down, Graham,' talk I thought it would be, it was more a, 'By the way, we'll be able to find out if it's got Down's syndrome tomorrow if we want'. That was it. Just a passing observation.

I'm still unsure, Diary. What if I'm not as caring as I think I am and I hit the red button before thinking it through? That the type of thing that can mess a man up for life. I did think about telling Alison that we should just leave it to nature, but she was so blasé about it, I didn't want to make a scene.

I'll sleep on it.

Monday March 12th 2012

I decided to tell Jane about the baby today. I need to take Wednesday off work for the first scan and thought I might be able to wangle the time off as carer's leave or something, rather than annual leave. I reckoned it was worth a try, anyway. I didn't think she'd have a problem with it, everyone else I've told so far has been overjoyed, but outwardly she didn't look overly pleased about the situation. Sometimes you can just tell when someone is being off with you and this was one of those times. Her words just didn't match her actions. She told me that she'd need to check with HR but she thought that I'd need to use my leave for it. I'm sure I saw her sneer as she headed out the kitchen.

Later she returned and confirmed that I would need to use my leave and that in future I needed to book time off in advance. I did point out that this was in advance, but she just raised her eyebrows. Before she could say anything else, though, she spotted Boris sneaking off out the kitchen and went off to drag him back in.

Tuesday March 13th 2012

8.00 a.m.

I had a dream last night that I dropped the baby. The baby was born and it was a little girl, I was trying to change her on the bed and she was rolling about, messing around, and I picked her up to stop her rolling off the side of the bed, then dropped her as she was wriggling. In the dream Alison came running just as I was picking the poor baby up. She wasn't moving. All of a sudden the room was filled with everyone I went to school with, my parents, the doctor and a couple of people I didn't know. They were all telling Alison what a bad person I was and how she should finish with me for killing her baby. I woke up just as I was being told to leave by everyone in the room. It was an awful dream and has haunted me all day. I hope it's not a premonition. I could be locked up for that sort of thing.

10.00 p.m.

Boris was sick in the kitchen today. I think he's definitely an alcoholic. Jane says he is one of the 'ethnics' she needs on her books to keep the Job Centre happy. If it was me I'd just get rid of him. Mind you, it was funny seeing him projectile vomit over the sandwiches as Jane sent him away from the food in the kitchen. The only place he could run to was the open dishwasher. I wouldn't have laughed if I'd been on washing up duty. Henry, who was, said it stunk of a mixture of burning tyres and brake fluid. I've no idea why he's still got a job. I wouldn't employ Boris.

I couldn't get the dream out my head today. It kept coming back to haunt me. I hope I have a better one tonight to take its place. It's just my luck, I never normally remember dreams, either.

Wednesday March 14th 2012

It was the twelve week scan today. I met with Alison outside the hospital. I had to rush from work as Jane said that I could only have two hours off. After I'd run there, which took forty-five minutes, I was close to collapse. I stopped running round the corner to try and look breezy and not like I was a complete nervous wreck when I got there. It didn't work, but I wasn't having a panic attack as Alison thought, I was just out of breath. It's a good job the waiting room chairs were near the door of the maternity unit. I just flopped into one while Alison went and signed in.

Being the NHS, we had to wait the obligatory fifty minutes after our appointment was due. I was late for work before we even went into the scanning room. Once we were in there, the midwife was lovely. I couldn't understand a word she said though, I think she just arrived from a Japanese nursing college a week ago, but I could see the little fish-looking baby on the grainy screen. It was swimming about as the midwife pushed the scanning machine over Alison's belly. I don't think the baby liked it as I could see the tiny hand batting away the intrusion before it darted off somewhere else to hide. The midwife would always find it, though.

Seeing the baby inside Alison for the first time was amazing. It's strange but I didn't *feel* a connection to my unborn, I felt *Wow*, but it wasn't a connection, like Alison talks about. I suppose it's different for her, though, as it is actually inside of her.

I was a bit disappointed that the midwife wouldn't even take an educated guess at the sex of our child, though. I'm fairly sure if I was to spend all day, every day, looking at little fish babies I'd be able to tell what sort it is. She wouldn't, though, she just kept shaking her head and saying 'no'. She did qualify the 'no' with something in the end, but I'm buggered if I know what she said.

When Alison first noticed the baby on the screen I heard a tiny little squeal of delight. Mother was seeing baby for the first time. We've not felt any kicking yet, but I'm sure last night when I put my hand on her belly I could feel something. Like a load of tiny little popcorn was going off inside. Probably the little one going ballistic kicking the walls, telling me to stop squashing it.

I heard the nurse say the words, 'Down's syndrome'. Alison just jumped in before I could say anything and asked her to check. What she did then was just zoom in a bit and start taking computer generated measurements of the skull of our child.

She mumbled something about seeing no problem and Alison translated to me later that they would be sending the images off for further tests to be done; however, this was normal and we shouldn't worry. The midwife is going to ring tomorrow or the next day and confirm what the tests say.

Alison asked the midwife lots of questions. I'd zoned out, though, and not just because I didn't understand the answers; it was more that I was focused on the TV screen in front of me that had my now calm son or daughter on it. 'Shim' was just lying there, moving her hand near her face like she was looking at it, wondering when the fingers would grow. I didn't need to wonder; I checked in my book and found out that the fingers are already there, they just need to get a bit bigger so they don't look like stumps. In fact, almost everything is there, so why they can't tell you if it's a boy or a girl, I don't know. Maybe if it's got a penis, it's just too tiny to tell. I hope if so and it's a boy, the poor little blighter is more blessed than I am. If it's a girl, then they don't have to worry about that sort of thing.

I didn't bother going back to work in the end. I phoned Jane from the corridor of the hospital (to get the background noise in) and said there'd been delays and that Alison had also come over all faint, so I was told by the doctor that I needed to stay with her. Jane didn't sound very happy about it, but there's nothing she can do, except put me on dishwasher duty and it's Friday tomorrow so everyone's a winner!

Thursday 15th March 2012

Something very strange happened at work today. Jane came up to me in the morning and said HR had told her that she would have to give me a warning for unauthorised absence. I reminded her that she knew I was going to the hospital and then told her that I'd gone as my wife is pregnant. This didn't sway her from her opinion though. In fact it seemed to make things worse, she just pursed her lips and walked off.

She was probably having a bad day.

Alison has a major craving for chips. This means I'm going to have to put up with Terry and his conversations about paintballing more often. I might see if I can find something on the Internet that says fried chips are bad for pregnant women so I don't have to get her them.

Friday March 16th 2012

I was at work when Alison called to say the Down's syndrome test had come back. When she said the words and as she'd called rather than waited till I was home, the cold sweat that instantly appeared on my back was so sudden I thought I might pass out. 'Yeah, so she says everything's alright, it's all clear,' she said, still oblivious to the anxiety I've had about this moment for the last couple of months.

So it's all OK, there is nothing to worry about, no decisions to be made. Now I've had a few hours to think about it, I'm glad I did all that worrying; maybe if I worry more about things, then the bad things won't happen. It seems to have worked out this time.

Saturday March 17th 2012

I was sitting in my chair tonight having just finished my second plate of Chinese food; Alison hadn't wanted any as it made her get acid. Anyway, Alison came striding into the room lifting her legs to her stomach and laughing. I asked what the problem was and she explained it was restless legs and it's caused by pregnancy. I couldn't understand why she was smiling as I remember when Keith was coming off some painkillers he used to have to take for his back, he got them and he used to be moaning all the livelong day about them.

I was thinking about it later and I have come to the conclusion that it's a testament to the strength of women. They are naturally strong and good-natured. Alison has gone up in my estimation as not just a good person, partner and lover, but also as tower of strength. Apart from that one night when she came here drunk, all I've seen from her is calmness.

Seeing how she dealt with it made me realise I love her. I hope she loves me back. We haven't said it yet.

Sunday March 18th 2012

I met Bill and Sue, Alison's parents, today. I hadn't planned on it, but as I've actively avoided it for almost a month now, Alison took matters into her own hands and arranged to meet them in a local carvery. They are nice people, which, having now fully fallen in love with Alison, I'm not surprised about.

The only bit that didn't go well was when I dropped my huge

plate of unlimited veg on the way back to the table. It was my own fault for putting so much gravy and cheese sauce on the piled-high plate that it started to leak over the edge and burn my hands. I had two choices: speed up and get through the maze of tables and chairs to our table and put it down, or drop the plate there and then. I went for the former; I'm civilised, I'm not going to intentionally throw a plate of dinner over anyone. So I sped up towards our table, I was moving in between the other tables like a pro, weaving and winding. I was almost there when someone moved their chair back quickly as they were getting up – I tripped, tried to control it and slammed the plate down right at the feet of Alison's dad. It didn't help that I then started wiping the burning hot cheese sauce down myself. I looked like I'd been let out of somewhere for the day.

Gladly neither parent asked Alison if I was one of her patients and after I'd cleaned up as best I could in the toilet, along with her father who needed to wipe the mess off the bottom of his trousers, we were able to sit down and have a nice meal. Although people did keep staring at me and laughing when I caught their eye.

Alison's parents are OK with how things are, they've had time to adjust and seem much less excitable than my own parents. That might be because they'd just met me in the situation we were in.

We spoke about it like adults and they offered – like my parents – to help where they could. Alison's father is a driver for Tesco and her mum works at a local school signing in the latecomers and listening to parents' complaints. I told them about my job; I thought they'd look down their noses at me,

but they seemed impressed that I fed so many people a day …
although I can't help thinking it would have sounded better if I
hadn't had cheese sauce drying all down my front.

They asked if I had any hope for the sex of the child. That
wasn't the first time someone'd asked me, Boris wanted to
know if it was a boy, would I think about naming him Boris,
after him. I'd dismissed that instantly and tried to think about
other things as every time I thought about the sex, I thought
about that conversation with Boris and, seeing as it was
between the stalls in the toilet, I'd rather not remember it.

Alison's dad would like a boy and her mum, a girl. I think it's
universal amongst humans that they want whatever sex they
are. My parents were the same when we spoke about it later on
the phone.

I suppose I'd like a son, but I wouldn't want him to be all
hyperactive like I used to be before the doctor gave me the
pills that calmed me down. I was a right handful. Maybe it's a
trade-off, boys are a nightmare when they're young, but with
girls you get all the worry of their teenage years and that they're
going to end up with someone who can't carry their own
dinner to the table without throwing it all over the place.

Sunday March 25th 2012

Today I cooked us a bit of lamb. Apart from the burnt bits it
was nice. Alison wanted to eat early as her restless legs were
bad in the late afternoon. Over dinner we talked about the sex
of the baby. I've predicted a boy and she claims that she knows
it'll be a girl and that I'm completely wrong. I pretended that I
was indifferent about my prediction and that it was just a bit of
fun, but deep down, I'll be gutted if I'm not right.

Alison said she can feel the kicks now. I keep rushing over, but the little chap stops when I put my hand there. I'm being blanked out by my own baby – already.

Saturday March 31st 2012

Alison was in the bathroom for hours and hours this afternoon. I couldn't work out what she was up to. I thought, for a while, that she was upset with me and had gone in there for a cry. After half an hour I went up to check, but was shouted at as soon as I said, 'Alison?' so headed back down again. After two hours, Alison came down walking like she had hurt her leg. She wouldn't say what was up, though. I just carried on and cooked dinner. She clearly didn't want to talk to me because she completely ignored my questions.

9.30 p.m.

Alison went to bed early tonight. I looked on the Internet and found out that pregnant woman suffer with constipation fairly badly, in some cases. This must have been what was bothering Alison today.

I'm not sure, but I think the fact that I was concerned enough to not only look for whatever problem it could be, but also to order some cream for her, means this is true love, like Romeo and Juliet the scat version.

There's a little bump poking out the front of Alison now; you can only just see it through her clothes.

APRIL 2012

Thursday April 5th 2012

Alison is getting a lot of problems with her legs. Boris says when his wife was pregnant that he used to have to massage them for her. I think I'll wait until I'm asked before I do that task. I was told once that my massages are a bit like being beaten up by a small child or midget.

The kicks are proper boots now. There is no mistaking it. I've felt it for myself, so Alison isn't lying about it. The last three nights the baby has kicked before Alison went to sleep, but I've not been there as she's been in bed early. Tonight was different though, there was a full on kick-off at tea time. It was a special moment to feel the baby inside.

It's an amazing thing that we humans can grow inside one another. Males can't, but females have both and men and women grow inside them. I'm not sure how alien warlords procreate, something weird, probably, but how we do it is amazing. All the male needs to do is something he loves doing anyway and the female body, over nine relatively short months, makes a complete baby. I started thinking about this tonight and had to stop. It's just such a huge event and wonder of nature, I felt overwhelmed.

Saturday April 7th 2012

I've found myself feeling Alison's belly in the night while she sleeps. I am normally much later than her at turning in so she's asleep when I get there. It feels a little like I'm abusing her, but there's nothing like that going on, I'm just connecting to my child. The last two nights I've put my hand there and I've had a little acknowledgement by way of a kick. Last night it woke Alison up. I got scared that it would be my fault so I quickly pretended I was asleep.

Tuesday April 10th 2012

Work was dreadful today. Jane stuck me on dishwasher duty as I was late. Alison was feeling faint when I got up so I couldn't very well leave her alone. I managed to get some food down her, followed by a couple of pints of water, and she felt much better. I didn't want to have an argument, but she would have been fine if she'd eaten breakfast.

Jane said she wasn't prepared to let me have more time off than any of the others. She said this despite me only being twenty minutes late and Boris regularly taking an hour to sit down in the toilet and talk to whoever is unlucky enough to use the cubicle next to him. It's got silly, lately, too; last time I was in there he started showing me pictures from the car magazine he was reading under the partition wall.

I didn't say anything to her, but I'm starting to get a little bit annoyed with Jane. I think it's because I have my own ideas and am not a complete moron, like most people she's ever managed, that she doesn't like me. I've had managers like that before. They have little qualification other than a name badge that says 'manager', they're completely unpredictable in mood, and they just like telling others what to do. It just depends on the day as to whether it's done politely or not.

I spent the rest of the day at the dishwasher, ignoring everyone in the kitchen and thinking about what I could make Alison for tea that wouldn't set her off. I finally decided on salad as it was a hot day. Then, when Jane had gone off for what she called a managers' meeting (but we all know it's an appointment at the hairdressers) I plated up a couple of ham salads and put them in my bag. It's not stealing, as we all do it and everyone is OK with it.

Thursday April 12th 2012

I woke up in the night to the most horrendous noise. I'd been dreaming that I was being chased by a hippo. The noise that woke me up told me that there was either a hippo or a helicopter in the room. Alison has wind and indigestion. Her burps are something I would have been so proud of when I was a teenage boy. Now, however, I wasn't so much proud as terrified. It took ages to get back to sleep, so I rubbed Alison's back until she dropped off then got up and stayed up watching the news on the Russian channel. It's quite interesting; they report all sorts of things I wouldn't know about from the UK news. This morning there was a report on how many Russians come to the UK then go home again as they don't think it's a nice place to live. Their gripe isn't the weather, like most people, it's the people. The people interviewed said they think

Russians and Britons are incompatible.

That goes some way to explaining Boris.

Saturday April 21st 2012

I asked Alison outright if she was living with me now today. I didn't mean it to be rude, I've gotten used to her being here now, she is still thinking about it apparently.

Little else to report today other than one of the longest waits in the world for a pizza to be delivered. The delivery guy must have known how shoddy he'd been as he didn't lurk around looking awkward after he'd handed over the boxes, like his sort always do.

Sunday April 22nd 2012

This morning's wake-up call was Alison blasting Mozart as loud as her phone would let her play it. Apparently babies start to hear around this time. I'm not sure that the first thing I'd want to hear is some boring old classical music. In fact, I definitely wouldn't. I think I'd have liked the first bit of music I listened to to be something like Bob Marley, Don't Worry, Be Happy. I should imagine that being a baby is fairly worrying. One day you can't see, a week later you've grown a pair of eyes.

I drifted off to sleep again once I'd got over the initial shock.

Later I rang Mum and asked her if she used to play me music. After umming and ahhing for a bit she asked if The Archers counted. Then she confirmed that she hadn't, but she was always near a radio anyway. She did say that my dad used to make monkey noises to me while I was still inside. This must explain something, surely.

I told Alison and she laughed. She said that it didn't matter what the noise was from the father as the baby gets used to the two main voices in its life. She then asked me to start talking to her stomach.

I don't mind telling you, Diary, I didn't want to and made the excuse that I needed to go to the toilet, which is an old favourite I have happily been using since the eighties. Alison laughed as I jogged off upstairs. I could hear her calling after me, something about being scared. I wasn't though, I just felt uncomfortable not being able to see the person I was talking to. I'm not that good on the phone, either. It's normally just a brief sharing of information and then a quick hang up. I don't go for hour long conversations about what I've been thinking about for the last half hour or anything like that.

Later on I could hear Alison upstairs; she was talking to her belly. I'm not one for calling people mental, but really, I'm not sure whoever it is in there is going to be able to understand English when they're only seventeen weeks old. Surely it takes a bit longer and besides, she already told me that it didn't matter that my dad used to make monkey noises as I couldn't understand.

I suppose it does bring her closer to the baby and cuts down on the chances of her going all crazy and killing it. There's been a few things in the news recently about mothers who get so depressed after birth that they harm their babies, so if talking to her belly helps then, regardless of how silly I think it is, I'm going to support her.

By making monkey noises.

MAY 2012

Tuesday May 1st 2012

Alison woke me up this morning; the baby was kicking her and she wanted me to see it. Yes, SEE it. The bumps were huge. The baby must be really going mad in there and wanting to get out. It was like seeing someone locked in a sleeping bag trying to find their way out.

I've seen it twice today and Alison has taken to sitting with her iPhone ready, waiting for it to happen, so she can film it. So far she's missed it as she doesn't actually know how to use the camcorder function on the phone and by the time she's shouted me across to make it work the baby has stopped kicking.

Wednesday May 2nd 2012

I was at work when the video of the belly moving came through, God knows how much it cost to send a video via text, and I just know she hasn't sent it to just me. I instantly checked Facebook to make sure she hadn't uploaded it there. I don't want my baby all over the Internet before it's even alive. Alison is one of these people who doesn't mind posting what she's had for dinner on the Internet. I've looked at her page and all her mates coo around a plate of food, saying things like, 'Ooh, I love carrots,' and stuff like that. It's not something I do. All I've ever used Facebook for is the games (God damn *Candy Crush*) and for stalking down girls from school to see if they're ugly yet. Thankfully she hasn't posted it online.

I have to say though, it was a good video.

Sunday May 6th 2012

It's been in the back of my mind for a while, but as tomorrow is the day we find out the sex of the baby, I've been thinking about the sexes more and more. A girl should be OK for most of her childhood before all the worry comes in during her teens, whereas a boy, by all accounts, will be an utter nightmare from the word go. I'm not sure if I can handle a boy. I know I've been keen on a little me, but now I've read up about it, it's a worry.

I think the uncertainty is the biggest thing that's played on my mind. I'm glad that, all being well, tomorrow we'll both know what the next few years are going to be like.

10.00 p.m.

I'm to and fro on the girl/boy thing. It's like I have scales of opinion in my head and they're moving about like there's a couple of Sumo wrestlers on each side jumping up and down. One minute I am thinking how great it will be to have a son, then I'm switching to how much hard work it will be.

I need to sleep.

Monday May 7th 2012

It's a boy. I can't believe it; I was right. I might even have to start calling myself 'mystic Graham'. I did the obligatory two arms in the air celebration when the midwife, who could speak full English this time, told us she could see the penis, or, as she called it, 'winky' My celebration was perhaps a little self-indulgent, a point that I noted when Alison started to cry. It's her own fault for buying so many pink items and claiming to have a 'mother's instinct', although I felt it probably wasn't the time for pointing this out.

The baby wasn't moving around as much today as he had done at the last scan. He did seem to bat away the scope that was prodding him, though. I think I'd do that, too, if someone was prodding me as I tried to sleep. So he's just like his dad already.

As we left, I asked for a photo, I've seen hundreds of them on Facebook and had people shoving them in my face, expecting me to be as interested in their little blob as they are, but no one has ever mentioned that they cost five quid. Per print. Can you believe that? I mean, I don't even think Polaroids were that expensive back in the day when that was the only form of instant camera. That they charge that price for a print in the day and age of camera phones is shocking! (You're not allowed to use camera phones in the room they show you the ultrasound in, as apparently it interferes with the equipment, which is a lie as I had mine on and the equipment was fine. I wonder if they had a lie to roll out about not using them in the ultrasound room?)

I begrudgingly paid the five pounds for a print, then Alison made me spend another ten pounds on getting one each for both sets of grandparents. I could have bought a digital camera for that price. I know we have to pay for prescriptions, and although I disagree with it as I've paid taxes and National Insurance, we do it because if you're lucky it isn't that much … but for the photos of your first baby? You'd think a bit of tax money would go towards that. I wonder if they'd still charge you if they needed the print of it; if it did have Down's syndrome or something, would the fee still apply? Probably, knowing this crooked bunch of bastards. The prints aren't even that good. There is no choice of size. It's small or small, no frames, just a shitty little envelope with a picture of a cartoon elephant on it. If we were fatties I could sue for that. Defamatory, that's what I'd say it was. I asked Alison if my nose was big enough for someone to get away with calling me an elephant as an insult, but she said that piglet would be a better one. I stopped thinking about the daylight robbery that had just happened and started to wonder how 'piglet' had come out of Alison's mouth so quickly.

In the car on the way home Alison asked me if I was going to get a real job soon. When I asked her what she meant, she said that she didn't really envisage her child growing up with a parent that washed plates for a living and, regardless of me reminding her that I only did this on a Friday to get out of cleaning the fryer and frying the fish, she did have a point. Up until now, I've just done the easiest job that requires the least amount of qualifications for the most money that I can find. I don't want my son being at school on the day they ask everyone what their dad does for a living and him having to stand up and say I cook bacon or load a dishwasher. It's hardly the sort of place that I'd even want to take him into for the day, to have a look at where Daddy works. Meeting Boris is only something you should have to do if you're getting paid for it at. No one deserves having him inflict his breath on them for free. It's bad enough on minimum wage.

Surprisingly, I didn't find myself arguing with Alison about the job, which I would have done if I hadn't just had the experience of seeing my son. I agreed with her and we moved on to have what I think is the most grown up conversation I've ever had. Alison asked me what I enjoyed doing. Which stumped me for a bit, so she asked me what I *didn't* enjoy doing, which didn't stump me at all. I started out by listing every single little job that I had to do in my current role, I surprised even myself with how much I seemed to hate the job I'm in now.

'Why do you do it when you clearly hate it so much?' Alison asked, not unreasonably.

'No one likes their job,' I told her. 'They just do it for the money.'

'That's not true, I love my job,' she replied.

'Is that a lie?' I asked. Alison went on to inform me that she loved her job. Or at least she does when she's there. I knew they all used to go out for drinks in her last job, but I thought it was something they were forced to do. We never go out for drinks together. Boris doesn't need the excuse of 'being out' to drink, he does it at work. Jane is now on my list for the person I'd be least likely to talk to if I ever saw her anywhere other than work. I kind of have to talk to her there, but if I was given the option I'd cut out even that. And the rest of the kitchen team struggle with basic human communication and either grunt and point, or in the case of the chef, scream and throw whatever is closest whenever they need something.

We talked about what I could do instead, Alison asked me to pick the one thing I would like to do if I could do anything, and suggested that I don't think about the training or qualification element, just name my dream job.

'Easy,' I said, 'managing a homeless hostel.'

It's true, I did want to do that. I used to be friends with a homeless guy. When I was waiting for my bus home I always used to talk to him. He used to sit on the bench outside the bus station and that's where I'd have my last cigarette before I went inside to jump on the last bus home. Jerry was his name, he used to tell me about his life before he ended up on the street. He'd been in the navy, then working in a local council somewhere, I can't remember where, then one day he came home from work and his wife had left him, took his two children with her and moved to France with a man that used to work in Boots.

Things went downhill for Jerry after that. He stopped going to work. Didn't tell anyone, just stopped going, then the drinking started, which moved on to drinking things he found in the shed, eventually. The bank came and took the house off him, he'd not been opening letters or taking any notice of anything much, so he hadn't packed anything; just one day he had a house with all his things in and the next he was sat on the bench outside the bus station with a carrier bag of beer from the shop. He went from having everything he needed in life to living on the streets in less than a year. When he lived on the street, Jerry didn't talk to anyone about anything for five years. He said I was only one of about ten people he'd spoken to since the day his wife left. I'm not sure why he chose me to tell his story to, but he did. He used to say that he enjoyed talking to me. At the time I thought that was code for 'I enjoy the free fags you give me', but the more I think about it now, though, the more I realise that it must have been nice to have a few minutes every day to get out of the dark place he lived in, even if the motivation for that was getting something for nothing from me.

I never really talked about myself to Jerry, apart from telling him how bad my day was. He always did the same thing when I started to tell him about that, though; he used to look himself up and down then look back at me. It was his way of telling me to shut up. He'd never say it, though, he was too polite.

I stopped seeing Jerry when I left the job I was in at the time. I've seen him a few times since, still on the bench and still sitting alone. I've often thought about going to see him, but it's just one of those things that always gets moved back to tomorrow.

It's always been in the back of my mind that one day, when I grew up properly, I'd work with the homeless. I've just never got round to looking into it.

'You should really look into that, then,' Alison suggested when I'd finished telling her about Jerry.

And do you know what, Diary, I may just do that. Not tonight, though, I'm too tired from driving to the hospital and back, and I don't have to think about work for at least forty eight hours.

The subject of names wasn't something that Alison wanted to talk about tonight, ether, although she did definitely veto

Graham, Junior and Little G.

Tuesday May 8th 2012

I've stuck the scan picture to the fridge, but I keep getting up from the sofa to go and look at it. Alison walked past and told me that if I was looking for food I needed to open the fridge, which I thought was a cruel jibe to make when I was only taking an interest in my son.

I've tipped the photo of me and my mate Keith on holiday when we were eighteen out of the frame and put the picture of my son in. it looks good sitting on the window sill, better than the fridge, and I don't have to keep getting up to look at him.

Alison went to bed early tonight, I think she's still upset about having a boy.

I spent the evening thinking over names, I keep coming back to Graham in one form or another; I think Little Graham has a ring to it.

Wednesday May 9th 2012

I've been thinking … as we're having a boy, that means he's probably going to be hyperactive. I'm not sure how I'm going to handle that. I know there isn't anything we can do about it now, but I can clearly see now that all my talk of 'I want a boy' was ill thought out and based on nothing other than me wanting a little version of myself.

This time in two years' time I'll be chasing him around the place, up and down the stairs, and unable to leave anything of mine lying around.

I've had to make a list of positive reasons to have a son as I've started to think negatively about it.

The family name will get carried on

I can watch him play sport.

I could manipulate him to take up a sport that I like.

I won't have to worry about him as much as I would a girl.

I can teach him my sexist jokes when he's old enough to appreciate them.

I'll have a bit of solidarity in the toilet seat argument that seems to happen in every house.

We can laugh at farts together.

We can ride bikes for miles and miles in the summer.

I can't think of a nine, but I think I've done ever so well with the other eight so I don't need one.

See, we humans can be positive.

Saturday May 12th 2012

Alison spent the day trying to convince me that I need to change my job. I was getting fed up with agreeing in the end. I thought she was just talking, but it turns out she meant get the laptop out and start looking. I was glad when my parents turned up to see how we were, on their way to the shops.

It's great having a baby on the way. Both sets of our parents keep asking if we need anything. If we were to turn into a benefit claiming baby machine, I'd never have to do a big shop again.

Mum went and got us a few bits while Dad fixed the shower and then told us both about the new TV he'd brought for the lounge. What he really wanted to tell us was that he had the old lounge TV in the shed now. He's also planning an extension. Mum returned with more food than we'd asked for and also a few DVDs for us to watch. I made us all a few sandwiches, showing off the skills I've learnt in my job. I think they were all impressed.

The DVDs did the trick: when Mum and Dad left, Alison had forgotten about going on at me about jobs.

Alison has thrown in the towel and admitted we now live together. I'm glad she's decided as I can start pointing out to her which are my drawers and which ones she can have, rather than her just borrowing mine all the time.

Sunday May 13th 2012

The usual Sunday fear of how crap the working week in front of me was about to be crept its way into my afternoon just after lunch. I started to think more and more about working in a hostel, I mean, I might not be able to swan into a management job at a hostel, but surely I could be a minion if I went to college and learnt a little about it. There'd be less learning time for a normal job than there would a management position, surely.

I spent the evening Googling what I needed to work in a hostel. There is very little information about it on the Internet. Most organisations say that 'life experience' is enough. I found myself on a forum where someone suggested doing an interpersonal skills course as this would help me be able to talk to people and relate to them on their level, whatever that means. I looked at the college website and they don't have the course currently, but used to run it. I'm going to ring them tomorrow and see if they have any plans to start it again.

Monday May 14th 2012

It was the normal dull day in the kitchen today. I cooked the bacon then went onto serving the food when it was time for the cheese on toast to be made. It was the normal people getting the same thing they have every day for breakfast. It got me thinking about mundane lives. People get stuck in a rut and end up doing the same thing day in day out for the whole of their working life, the only reason I've avoided it up to now is I keep changing one shitty job for another.

On the way home I popped into the library to see if they had any books on working with people. I was going to take one out called *Homeless People and How to Work With Them*, but when I got to the counter the librarian told me I owed sixteen pounds for a couple of DVDs that I took back late seven and a half years ago. I asked if I could pay next time, when I brought the book back, but she wouldn't let me. So I sat in there and read for ten minutes before getting bored with the lack of sound and left vowing to hate the council run library for the rest of my days.

I also forgot to ring the college when I got home.

Alison knows when our boy is awake and when he's asleep now. It's amazing. He wakes up just as she is about to go to sleep and likes to kick for a while. Alison likes to call me to feel the kicks every night. More than once I get up there to nothing. I've decided I'm not going to go anymore as the baby is winning the battle of wits. I'm sure this is the first wind up from my son. I can see him now, laughing in there, made up that he's made me stop playing Xbox, run upstairs and navigate all the beanbags and pillows Alison has on the bed, only to find no movement.

Tuesday May 15th 2012

I went back to the library today and paid the fine, it means I can't save any money for my future son this week, but at least I can tell him I did the right thing.

I finally remembered to ring the college today; my heart sank when they said that they had no current plans to run another interpersonal skills course. However, they also said that as they've had some interest in the course over the last few weeks, they were going to have a meeting about it and that situation might change. I asked when they'd know for sure and the lady told me it was likely to be a couple of weeks, and to ring back to check.

It might not have been the lack of sound in the library that bored me the other day; that book on working with homeless people is really dull. It keeps talking about reports and different methods of counselling to 'engage' homeless people. I don't know what the word 'entrenched' means but they keep talking about it in the book. I could look it up, but I'm not sure I'll like what I find. It sounds like a trouser complaint.

Alison is going to stay with her parents this weekend so I have some time to myself. I might ask Keith if he fancies going for a few beers.

Saturday May 19th 2012

I feel so rough.

Sunday May 20th 2012

I'm just about feeling normal today. Keith came round on Friday and we went out. It was only the local, but once we started drinking, things got a bit out of control. Pint followed after pint, then it was port after port. I don't know why, but port is Keith's favourite drink. I have a vague recollection of being in a club and then in KFC, but that's about it. Mainly I remember, and can still taste, the port.

Today I spent the day just lying around. I may take up reading. I'm too old to go out on the town. It's not worth the trouble.

Wednesday May 23rd 2012

I got *War and Peace* out of the library today. I asked the librarian what was a good classic book to start with; she asked what my reading level was and I didn't know what she meant, so replied that it was excellent.

I'm going to start the book tomorrow. Tonight I just fancy watching the tele.

Friday May 25th 2012

War and Peace is awful. I read a whole five pages and there wasn't one murder, just some old bloke wandering around. It'd be far better if there was a horse and cart chase or something. This is now my Friday night. That and trying to get Alison comfortable with the various sized pillows that keep showing up in my house. I'm not sure where she gets them all from, people must bring them round as she doesn't go out.

Sunday May 27th 2012

The baby now has all the white gunk over him that'll make him waterproof and safe while he's still inside Alison. Boris told me that when the babies come out they don't let you wash them off before you hold them, you have to hold the baby with all the white stuff on them. I've Googled a picture of a newborn and I have to tell you, Diary, I wish I hadn't.

JUNE 2012

Monday June 4th 2012

7.00 a.m.

Alison woke up in the night with pains in her stomach; we phoned the hospital who suggested checking if there was blood. She did and there was. They recommended that we get to the hospital quick sharp. I drove Alison's car like I'd stolen it and, luckily, got us there without causing anyone any more bleeding.

A&E was packed, although the nurses on reception must have had word we were on our way as they told us to go straight through the waiting area and into the secret waiting area they don't tell the time wasters and broken leg brigade about. I made a mental note to remember this place. No sooner had I parked Alison onto a seat than another nurse came over and led us off into a side room. It must have been about three minutes from car to examination room.

I was asked to wait outside by the doctor who entered shortly after we had. It was for no other reason than there were now three of us standing over the bed where Alison lay and there just wasn't room for us all; seeing as I had the least medical qualifications, by rights it was me that had to stand outside the door. Well, curtain – which they promptly closed behind me.

I got bored and my legs hurt after about three minutes so I went back to the secret waiting area, which was just up the corridor a bit. I still wish I hadn't now, there was an old man that wasn't moving in a chair, and a teenager with his arm bent the wrong way at the elbow. It was worse than watching some of the videos I've had the misfortune to watch on Facebook before.

I ended up just hovering outside the examination rooms, although it took me two guesses to remember which one Alison was in. This was even more unfortunate, as I got to see someone's leg that was cut open from the ankle to the knee, like it had been unzipped. There was literally nowhere safe for me to stand to be away from such evil. It couldn't get much worse. Well, until I drew back the curtain on the room that Alison was in and saw what was happening in there. I'm not even going to do myself the damage of reliving it here, on paper. I backed out and went to the car park, where I smoked three of the four cigarettes I had left until my phone rang and Alison told me she'd been give the all clear and that it was just a bit of blood. She hadn't seen me when I walked into the room, so she was unsure where I'd got to. I was too tired to complain about my terrible night and just wanted to get home, so I took her back to the car we'd abandoned on the way in and we drove home.

Alison went straight to bed when we got in. I'd woken up during the drive and didn't feel like sleeping. I could have lost my son today. With all the gruesome sights I'd seen, I hadn't thought about the situation when we were at the hospital; it was when I was alone at home that it hit me. I've realised that I definitely want a son, there is no doubt whatsoever that I want to be a father.

I make a commitment to you and anyone that reads this book three thousand years in the future that I will find a different job and I will cut a good father figure.

I've had no sleep now and there is only an hour before I'm due to be at work.

10.00 p.m.

Work was awful today, I started feeling really tired just after we finished serving breakfast. Alison texted me throughout the morning to let me know how she was. She had a day lying around. No work again for her today.

I spent some time this afternoon wondering how good it would be to be a woman. I mean, during this pregnancy Alison has had at least five weeks off work, all here and there. I'd love to be able to ring in when I didn't feel like going to work and not be questioned as to why I wasn't going in. I've heard women talk about how much pain pregnancy is, but I don't think it can be that bad, Mother Nature wouldn't make it so that no one ever wanted to do it, or we'd run out of people, we'd simply stop having babies and the human race would die off. I'm sure as an alien warlord you've had genetic remodelling or something, but here we just have to reproduce the old way.

It would also be nice to use the toilet sitting down for everything without being called a tranny over the cubicle by Boris. He was in there today while I was hiding. I only needed a number one, but I went in the stalls just to sit down and take the weight off my feet. It's also not much of a break if you just stand somewhere other than you were standing before, and seeing as they don't have anywhere to sit in the warehouse (which is the only other place to hide) it was the toilet that got the pleasure of my company for my afternoon rest. I didn't stay as long as I normally would, as once Boris had finished name calling over the cubicle wall he started being sick. It didn't help my relaxation.

I picked up a nice curry for us both on the way home. Alison was pleased with it and wolfed it down. I asked her if she'd eaten anything all day. She hadn't. We then had a bit of a row about how she needed to eat. I felt bad afterwards and apologised, but then we had the same row again. I made her a load of sandwiches and left them in the fridge. I'm in the spare room tonight, as Alison said she didn't want to sleep in the same bed as someone as selfish as me.

Tuesday June 5th 2012

I'd booked today off so I made sure I was ready with breakfast in the morning for Alison, fruit salad and a bowl of cereal. I even went out for bread so she could have toast.

Alison wanted a lazy day today, but I managed to convince her to come for a walk in the park with me this morning. It was hot so we didn't stay out long. It was nice to break the day up, though. I asked Alison if she had any fear about having a boy; she said she didn't mind what sex it was as long as it had all its fingers and toes. I did ask what would happen if it was missing one finger or if one was shorter than the rest, but Alison just told me to stop being silly.

I made a chicken salad for lunch then we watched a film this afternoon. Being rushed into hospital doesn't seem to have fazed Alison. She's taking it all in her stride. I know she was worried on the day and that the examination wasn't a nice thing to go through, but I'm noticing more and more how emotionally intelligent and strong she is as a person. I'm not; I'm a nightmare. Alison being as staunch as she is makes me realise how emotionally unstable I am.

The midwife, Bev, popped round just before tea. She had heard that we were in hospital the other night and said she wanted to assure Alison that she was OK and that there wasn't anything to worry about; she stayed for almost an hour talking to Alison. I busied myself in the kitchen, making tea and looking out of the window. I didn't want to get involved too much in the conversation, just in case the topic went back to whatever it was they were doing in the cubicle at the hospital.

Before Bev left she popped her head into the kitchen. I was still looking out the window with a sink load of washing up in front of me that I had been too distracted to do. Once I knew she was there I pretended to have just been pausing for a moment and got back to washing dishes. I felt like I was in trouble. I didn't want to get told off, so I just kept saying 'Just a moment' every time she tried to speak. When I'd finished drying my hands, I allowed Bev to speak by shutting up and giving her eye contact for the first time.

'I just wanted to assure you that everything is OK and that you're doing all you should be,' she told me, coming closer.

I'm not good in emotional moments.

'I know that being an expectant father can be hard,' she added, rubbing my arm.

I wasn't sure how to respond, so I thanked her for letting me know and started moving towards the kitchen door. It wasn't that I was being rude, Diary, it was that I didn't want to cry in front of her. Sometimes when someone speaks about the very thing that has caused you to panic, then it brings it all back, which occurred as soon as Bev focused on what had happened the other night. It took me at least fifteen minutes to remember that I'd been washing up before Bev came to see me, by which time the water was cold and I had to go student on the job. It's just the same as hot, only you have to scrub harder.

This evening I tried a different tack and asked Alison again what she thought the best thing about having a boy would be. Alison just smiled and said that he'd be her little man.

It will be pretty cool to have a little man running about the place.

I've decided that I project too much. I think about and worry about things that are too far in the future to do anything about. I'm not sure how to stop doing it, but there must be a way. Not everyone does it. Alison is very good at just living in the day; she is happy with it too.

Tonight I've been worrying about being worried about everything. It's a circle that I need to break. I did do some Internet searching this evening, but it didn't help … I just found myself on a load of depression forums with all the miserable people who are talking about similar, but not the same things. I'm not depressed, I'm just different. I'm going to ring the doctor's in the morning and see if there is anything they can do to help me; I can't be the only person in the world that has this problem. Surely it doesn't mean I'm depressed, like the people I came across this evening.

Monday June 11th 2012

Living with a pregnant person has very few benefits. Being made to sleep on your own sofa is one of the low points. The last couple of weeks have been up and down, Alison has been at work when I get home so I've had a couple of hours to myself most days. I hope there's no more arguments to come. We've not rowed since the other week and I've managed to get her to eat at least two meals a day. She won't have breakfast no matter how much I nag as she says waking up pregnant is only comparable to waking up with a hangover.

I have now spoken to the college again and I am signed up for the interpersonal skills course, which is to run in January. They've decided not to run it in September. I've paid the minimum deposit and won't be able to save this week, but it's booked and all I have to do is make sure I pay the rest of the £300 fee before it starts. I've got it all worked out and if I ride my bike to work instead of taking the bus, then I can still afford to save £20 a week and cover the college. I'll also have to cut out buying chocolate bars, but then if I'm on my bike I won't be walking past any shops so unless I'm painfully addicted, I'll be okay. I don't think I am, but I'm sure I'll find out soon enough.

I've just realised that I am sounding more and more grown up. I'm not sure how I feel about this. Maybe I should go out with

Keith and re-live my youth again.

Thursday June 14th 2012

My birthday.

So I'm now twenty-nine. This time last year I was just about to go on holiday on my own. I didn't go in the end. I got as far as the airport, but decided that it was just too loser-ish to go on my own. It seemed like a great idea when I booked it, but I just got so panicked that the check in assistant would know I was going on my own, regardless of the story I'd concocted about meeting someone when I got to Ibiza. I'm glad I didn't go in the end as I read in the paper that the week I'd planned to have been there was the worst rate for holiday makers dying on the isle recorded on file. I might not have seen my birthday.

It's strange to think that I've had such a big change in a year. I'm used to changing jobs. In fact, I don't think I've ever had the same job on any of my birthdays that I had the year before. Having both a girlfriend and a baby is massive, though. I've been thinking more and more about whether I love Alison or not. Today I decided to put that to the test and think about how I'd feel if she wasn't here. I had a dream last week about her dying whilst giving birth. The thought of that happening hasn't left me. Today I purposefully gave more thought to the dream than I have done in the past. Before I'd just pushed it away, today it felt like I needed to give the thought some brain time. It's like it won't leave me unless I consider the possibilities and it's once I had done that and felt the projected feelings that Alison dying would make me feel, that I knew, I just *knew* that I loved her. It's a strange feeling and not something I'm sure I can put into words; hopefully whoever is reading this is human and not as much of a loser in love as I was before meeting Alison. What I do know is that it isn't like a light switch that is flicked. The feeling isn't like taking a pill and feeling the results within a few minutes. In my case, I had a niggling, I needed to run through a few scenarios in my head to see what my reaction was. It sounds silly, but it is just something that I knew I needed to do. I've never thought that way before. I suppose it is just a process that goes through people's minds when they are falling, or have fallen, in love. As humans we're logical beings and love is kinda illogical. We're selfish and love isn't.

I'm getting emotional thinking about it now as I have never felt this way about anyone before. We're not going out tonight as Alison is self-conscious about the way she walks, plus she's been feeling really tired. I think I'll tell her tonight.

10.00 p.m.

I was sitting eating my birthday tea (ham and pineapple pizza) tonight. Alison didn't have any as she's been told by the midwife that she has been eating too much rubbish and that the baby is in danger of being diabetic if she carries on. Anyway, I was eating my dinner and I decided that it was time to tell her. I'd been thinking about how I was going to do it all day.

In the end I said, 'It's a cracking pizza, love.' I thought she'd get the meaning in what I said, but she didn't.

She just said. 'The 1970s called, they want their language back,' and laughed.

I still haven't told her how I feel. I might not even do it until our boy arrives. Maybe I just need to pick a moment when I haven't got pizza all round my face.

JULY 2012

Wednesday July 18th 2012

Alison and I talked about antenatal classes tonight. I'm a modern man, so I'll go along and show everyone that I'm willing to help. She then told me the class was tomorrow and I felt like I'd been tricked into it, but seeing as I had nothing else planned and I couldn't think of anything fast enough, we're going.

Things are getting real now. I can't quite put into words how I'm feeling. I'm OK most of the day, then sometimes I'll just get a completely overwhelming feeling of joy, closely followed by a crushing fear of how we're ever going to manage or afford it.

Thursday July 19th 2012

The first antenatal class was tonight. I was a bit annoyed that there were two other couples waiting outside who'd got there before us, I wanted to get there first and show the nurses running it that we were the most keen to learn. I did manage to drag Alison in front of the couple just leaving the car park as we arrived, so we at least got to the door before them.

There were a few pleasantries exchanged and bumps stared at, then we all filed into the Mother and Baby Centre. It's only about three streets from my house, but I didn't even know it was here. I've lived here almost ten years and thought I knew the area pretty well, but it seems that unless it's something I'm interested in – a shop, a pub or something shiny or bright – then I don't notice it at all. There is a massive sign above it, too, so it's clear what it is. I've just not taken it in before. I'll have to up my game in the paying attention front as I'll have a baby to consider. I can't go about not noticing danger in the street or things in the house that he could put in his mouth. I'm going to get a book on keeping focused on my surroundings out of the library this week.

We were five minutes early, as were the three other couples. The other seven seemed to have a more cavalier attitude to time keeping and came in dribs and drabs until half past seven. I can't bring myself to walk in anywhere half an hour late, I'd rather not go if I'm that late, but some people have no such shame. If I had my way, latecomers would be made to wait in the car park until everyone else had finished and then told to come back another day. Sadly it's not my world, though, and people don't do as I say. Maybe in the world you're living in, this could be something you could implement. If you haven't already, that is.

The session itself was just as bad as I thought it would be: a dreary nurse read from a book that should have been posted to us before the session, but wasn't because apparently they've run out of money and can't print them anymore. Apparently it is cheaper to gather us all in a room and read it to us like we were babies.

There wasn't any of the sitting on the floor, breathing with the partners that you see on TV and most of the blokes just looked bored. I intentionally put on the most bored face I could in the hope that the nurse would see it and realise she was boring. She carried on regardless, mostly talking about what it's like to be in the hospital and what you're allowed to take in with you.

She then spent the last two hours talking about breast feeding. This was also supposed to be on a DVD that was sent to us beforehand, but – you guessed it – they'd run out, so we watched a VHS version that she had. The video had eight women on it and after each point was made, each of the eight women was interviewed and fed back the exact same answer as the seven others. The message was *breast feed your baby for as long as you can manage to because it is better for them*. It really didn't need to be a ninety minute video. I'm fairly sure it was only that long because they felt the need to find women of every ethnicity to feed back. It's a PC world gone mad and I was bored. Did I mention that?

Even the double kebab on the way home didn't make me feel better about the colossal waste of time the evening had been. The very worst thing about it is that we have to go back next week, and the week after, for more of the same.

Friday July 20th 2012

Alison has finished work today. They've let her take her time more before the baby than after. I wish I could give up work now.

Sunday July 22nd 2012

Today Dad came round and helped me start turning the spare room into a nursery. All the old wardrobes needed taking down, I was good at this. Sometimes there is nothing better than going apeshit with a hammer and smashing things up. Putting up the new ones and the cot was a different story altogether and made me wish I'd saved smashing the old ones up. We managed to get all the furniture made. The painting was the easy bit, it took up time but we didn't have to try and make out any instructions written by Mexicans. Alison had long since gone to bed by the time we finished, but didn't mind when I woke her up to look at our handiwork. She wasn't as interested in having a conversation about my dad's tool belt as he was, though.

All in all, the men have done their work today. It feels good. Well, not my back, that hurts to hell, but inside I feel like I've accomplished something. I've made a room for my baby. I'm getting to be a real dad.

Thursday July 26th 2012

Tonight was the second antenatal class and they showed us the most horrendous video I've ever seen. And I've looked on Rotten.com. It was a no holds barred birthing video and, like last week, they'd filmed as many of the people from the breast feeding video as possible. I saw all sorts. Keith told me that I should stay up at the head end, which I'd planned to do. Unfortunately the luxury of choice was taken away from me tonight. Once I spotted the hair I started to look at the clock. Watching my life tick away was much more preferable to watching the horror that was taking place on the screen.

At home I asked Alison about a caesarean. 'C-section, you mean?' she said, showing that she'd been listening much more than I had. 'They'll keep me in for ages if I have that, plus there's a huge scar. I'd rather not.'

I've scribbled out the part I added to the birthing plan while she was in the bathroom.

Saturday July 28th 2012

We're in a heatwave. The last couple of nights have been so hot I've taken to sleeping on the floor in the spare room. Alison is really uncomfortable anyway, but the heat is making her moan far more than she normally does. In fact, I've never heard anyone go on so much about being hot. I've had to consult my book for the first time in ages. There was a handy tip about putting ice cold water into a hot water bottle and putting it at the bottom on the bed. Apparently the blood that then shoots up the body back to the heart is cooler. I volunteered to go and pick up Alison's bottle. She's been lying down most of the day and she says it's helped, but is still too hot. The fan is on 24/7. I wish we were rich enough for air con.

The kitchen at work has been fairly unbearable, so I know what Alison feels like. However, at work they have to provide us with ten minute breaks every hour and as many free cold drinks as we like. I'm fairly sure if it were left up to Jane, we'd get nothing.

Monday July 30th 2012

The heavens opened today, and along with the rain that fell from the sky, so did a cooler atmosphere, not only in the weather, but in the house. Alison is much more comfortable. I was at work when the rain fell, I'm sure it was hail too. I couldn't see as I was serving up lunch, so can only go by my ears. Even chef smiled when we heard it was raining.

AUGUST 2012

Thursday August 2nd 2012

The third and final night of sitting and listening to the midwife at antenatal tonight. It wasn't as bad as last week, we just sat around and listened. She told us what we would and wouldn't be allowed to take in: some hospitals allow you to take wipes, others don't. We were advised to go and have a look at the ward before the birth. I'm not sure I fancy that. I think I'll just locate the toilets and the canteen when we're there. I don't think we need to be shown round a smelly old, noisy hospital. They also explained to us about all the different money-off vouchers they could have given us if they hadn't run out of magazines. We can print them off the website though. Seriously, the whole antenatal classes set up should be put online. If they want to save the money they spend on midwives, DVDs and magazines they run out of, they might as well just email you a video of the midwife talking and then you get to watch all the other videos, read the book that they read out, and print off your vouchers. I reckon you could do it in an evening.

They did explain what the point was of the Centre we were sitting in and it did sound good. When I'm at work, Alison will be able to pop in there and have sessions with the little one. They do all sorts. The one that interested me was baby massage, though, apparently babies really like all that. It helps them to move around the food and air that's inside them. They also do a swimming club that all the little people can go to after eight weeks. I might even see about taking the little chap to that myself. I like a good swim.

Alison enjoyed the evening, although she did say that seeing me out the corner of her eye looking at the ceiling and sighing put her off a bit.

Friday August 3rd 2012

I spoke to Jane about paternity leave today. She said I was only allowed two days, then I had to use my holiday. This is wrong. I checked the Internet and in the UK men are allowed two weeks off and this has to be paid at the statutory rate of about £90 a week. I couldn't be bothered to argue with 'she who knows it all', though, so I just went and spoke to Mary in HR who told me all I had to do was let her know the expected dates I'd be off and she would sort out the rest. She even asked if I wanted to take any holiday as well. I won't though, I'll need to use my annual leave days for Christmas.

Saturday August 4th 2012

Alison and I went to her parents for lunch today. I'd like to say I was surprised to find my father in the garden advising Alison's dad on what shed he should buy, but I'm not. They've been getting closer and closer recently.

Over lunch we started talking baby names. Bill thinks he should be called Bill. Sue is more going for Charles. Mum thought we should go with something like Gary. I saw Alison visibly shake when she heard that. I have to agree, Gary and Graham do not go well together. I can see the Christmas cards now. Alison was strangely quiet during dinner. I found out why when I got home.

Alison was emotional. She said that she'd been thinking about the name Charlie and because my mum had suggested it, she felt bad as she didn't think she'd be a good mother if she couldn't even name the baby before someone else did.

I have a confession to make, Diary. I didn't know what to say or do while she was lying in bed and crying, so I said I'd make us a drink and I took half an hour longer than I should have. I went for a smoke and tried to figure out the female mind at the same time.

I must have looked mental as someone outside asked me if I was OK. When I said I was and that I was just thinking, they replied that if I thought any harder the lines in my forehead would stay where they were. Being insulted by a stranger made me come to my senses, so I went back in, showered, and went and hugged Alison as she cried herself to sleep. I've still no idea what was up with her.

My book did say that women's emotions are all over the place when they're pregnant.

Tomorrow I think I'll tell Alison that Mum may have said it first but there is no way she would have thought of it before she did. That should work.

I actually quite like Charlie. Charles sounds rubbish and just to show Alison that I like her idea more, I'll tell her that we will call our son Charlie on the birth certificate. That'll work, I'm sure of it.

Sunday August 5th 2012

When I spoke to Alison about names at breakfast she'd completely forgotten about how upset she was yesterday. She even remarked that Charlie must be a good name if both she and my mother had thought of it.

We've agreed on Charlie.

I made popcorn later this afternoon. Alison told me later tonight that it had bunged her up. I think our sexual relationship is on hold now.

Monday August 6th 2012

I was right, of course, I am allowed two weeks off; Jane looked like she was going to throw something when I arrived back at the kitchen after speaking to Mary in HR. She was still on the phone and threw me the daggers. Seriously, if looks could kill, that one would have taken a chainsaw to me and my family. Later I heard her shouting at Boris in the storeroom. She was banging stuff about, she'd probably caught him sleeping in there again. Either that or he'd been at the cooking wine again.

Tuesday August 7th 2012

Alison was up in the night with her restless legs. I woke up to find her doing a pregnant version of *Riverdance* around our bedroom at 3 a.m. She said she'd been up for an hour by then, so I tried to persuade her to have a bath, but she wouldn't. She doesn't like baths. I offered to help her get in and out, but she sent me back to sleep.

Work was bad today. Jane is in one of her moods. It wasn't my fault I was late; I slept in. My alarm went off, but I'd taken my phone into the kitchen when I'd made a drink in the night and didn't hear it going off. She didn't say anything to me today, but says we'll talk about it on Friday before we knock off for the weekend.

Friday August 10th 2012

Jane was slamming about at work all day, telling me what to do, even though I was already doing the jobs that she was telling me I had to do.

I was hoping she'd forgotten about meeting up before the end of the day as I wanted to get home and make sure Alison hadn't gone through the floorboards while trying to rid herself of restless legs. I was almost out the door when she called me back.

Apparently I am on my final warning from her. If I am late or do not attend work again for whatever reason, she says she'll have to speak to HR. She said that she will be thinking about what to do with me over the weekend and that I should prepare myself for a tough week next week.

Just like Jane to tell me that on a Friday and completely ruin the weekend for me.

I can't think of anything else. What if I lose my job completely and can't find another one? I've never had to listen to people talk to me like this before, but as I'm now having to make sure we do have money coming in I've got to learn to put up with it. I'd have never even let her get past 'I thought we were meeting' if the situation was different. I'd have told her where she could shove her deep fat fryer. I might have even called *her* a deep fat fryer.

I didn't tell Alison. She doesn't need anymore to worry about.

The restless legs seem to wait until she is ready to go to sleep before they attack her. She still won't have a bath though.

I spent the evening trying not to think about what could happen next week at work. My head kept taking me back to the conversation with Jane. I know that she shouldn't have spoken to me on a Friday like that, no good manager would. Jane isn't a good manager, though, and she wanted me to feel terrible all weekend. That was her plan and it looks like it's going to work and I don't know how to stop thinking about it. I think I'm more upset that I allowed myself to be spoken to like that.

11.20 p.m.

Alison finally tried having a bath this evening. She said it helped while she was in there, but not after, so couldn't see the point of doing it again. I was too caught up thinking about work and snapped at her for having the gall to speak while my head was in a mental argument with Jane.

That's the second night in a week that Alison has gone to bed crying. I'm not proud that tonight it was me that caused it.

Saturday August 11th 2012

I woke up early this morning; I wanted to get up and make Alison breakfast. Alison wasn't interested, though, and was up and dressed before I got out the bathroom. She said she was going to her mother's for the day and then left without saying anything more.

I sat around all morning trying to think of a way out of the situation I'm in at work. I know some of it is my fault, but I also know that I shouldn't be spoken to the way the Jane speaks to me. In between thinking I kept having mental arguments in my head with Jane. I have planned out every way that Monday can go. Unfortunately, I can't actually say what I've planned out as I'll lose my job and until I've sorted college out I need it.

Alison returned this evening after not replying to my text messages all day. I knew she'd read them as there is a little bit in the text box that tells me when they've been opened.

She was still in her mood. I tried and tried to sort things out, but she was still frosty before she went to bed. I couldn't bring myself to tell her that I could be losing my job. The book says that any amount of stress is not good for the baby or the mother so there is little point adding to the stress I've already caused by snapping at her.

I'm hoping it'll pass as I want to put my hand on her belly and connect with my son.

Sunday August 12th 2012

Alison was fine this morning. It seems she'd dished out a

sentence of one day's silent treatment and that has now passed.

She wants me to start talking to the baby. I haven't said anymore than 'hello' yet and it feels weird, talking to her belly. I asked her if she had yet and she said she was doing it all of yesterday with her dad. He was singing to her belly, too, apparently.

There's nothing in my book about talking to the belly. I'm going to take one star off the glowing review I had planned to write for it.

Maybe tomorrow I'll feel more comfortable talking to her belly; at the moment I'm happy with the little kicks I get back most of the time I put my hand on there.

Monday August 13th 2012

Jane wasn't in today, she had one of her made up 'meetings' that she tells us about before coming into work the next day with new hair and nails. She's so selfish. I've got another night's worrying to do. Boris looked disappointed, too, when we got the message from chef that she wouldn't be in. Mind you, chef does throw more stuff at Boris when Jane isn't there; I'd be disappointed, too, if I knew I was in for a day of being a target.

Tuesday August 14th 2012

Jane was in today. She didn't mention anything about HR. I was getting wound up with how she'd been on Friday, threatening me and ruining my weekend, only to not even bother to show up on Monday. Just before we were due to leave, I asked her if there was anything more coming from HR and she looked at me like she didn't know what I was talking about, then laughed and said not to worry about it as she walked out, taking her new hair with her.

Saturday August 18th 2012

We're down to the final month count down now. Alison is taking pictures of herself and her bump in the mirror. I've got a sense of impending doom. She's got her midwife appointment next week; after that they'll see her every week. She's going on her own now as it's getting to the point where it's more and more intimate and she's still embarrassed about that stuff. I don't mind. I can't take more time off work anyway and to be honest I always feel like a spare part in those situations.

The birth could realistically be any day now though.

Sunday August 19th 2012

I asked Alison today if she's got her overnight bag packed. She hadn't and it took me all afternoon to motivate her into doing it. I did offer to begin with, but all that seemed to do was motivate Alison to point out a list of my weaknesses. Not just packing weaknesses, either, general life ones.

The bag is packed now, though, and we're ready for the off. I've checked the car tyres and have made sure there's enough petrol in to get us to the hospital and back again. I think that's everything I need to be prepared.

Wednesday August 22nd 2012

Alison has had her midwife appointment today, and they've filled her in as to how it will go. As we approach the 11th

September, she'll have access to the mobile number of the midwife. We thought she already had that, but it turns out there's another one that they actually answer, saved for when the time comes. She was told that if she's not had it by the time the due date comes, they'll be round that day to check on her, then again seven days after that. If they haven't seen anything like movement on the second visit, they'll book her in there and then for inducement, which is when they kickstart things for us. They don't like to leave the baby in there for longer than ten days past due date for first-time mothers. I'm not sure Alison could take much more than the due date without the skin on her belly just splitting. She is massive now. Her mum's been round most days helping out as she can't go out the house on her own. She gets tired at the drop of a hat and it can come on at any time. It's not safe to be out alone.

Friday August 24th 2012

Boris was so drunk at work he fell asleep in the toilet. I could see his trousers poking under the bottom of the cubicle. I didn't report him to Jane, it's not my job to keep tabs on him. To my disgust though, when it came to time to get the fish in the fryer, she just told me to do it. I couldn't complain without telling her where Boris was and I've learnt not to do that as she'll only find some way of blaming me. When Boris still wasn't back after serving I had to load the dishwasher with all the plates and then scrub the pots and pans, which had food all dried on as they'd been left. I didn't see Boris until I was leaving; he had somehow managed to get himself a lift home in Jane's car.

I'm glad it's Friday.

Sunday August 26th 2012

We're nearing the two week period. There's been no twitches or anything, despite everyone we've ever known asking every five minutes.

I'm not that fazed about it. It's still in the incomprehensible stage. I know it's only a matter of weeks away, but I've never been through it before so I don't know what's coming and I think I've got the type of brain that just blocks things like that out and puts them in the 'I hope it's OK' part of my mind. I'll probably just start panicking one day and have to be given a brown paper bag.

Both sets of parents were round today, all trying to find something to do to help. There wasn't much they could do except relax and stop stressing us out. Alison's mum offered to be there at the birth; I was a little annoyed about this, I mean it's like blatantly saying to my face that I won't be able to cope. Surely it can't be that hard just standing there and encouraging Alison to do her best? In the end they bought us dinner from the Chinese and then went home.

I'm still a little miffed at Alison's mum. I didn't tell Alison, even when she asked what was up with me later. There's no point rocking the boat.

SEPTEMBER 2012

Tuesday September 4th 2012

One week to go. Alison went to the midwife's yesterday who said the head looked like it was engaged (pointing down) so there is some sign of movement, but not twinges or anything. Alison has taken to lying in bed almost all day. The only time she moves is to get food or to go to the bathroom. Her bladder is like that of an old woman. I think this upsets her more than anything else, it takes her a while to find a way to lie comfortably, then once she's done that she's got about five or ten minutes before she needs to get up and empty her squashed bladder.

Work is getting worse. There's nothing Jane won't do or say if she thinks it'll make me feel bad. Today she was talking about how bad the local hospital is. She wasn't talking to me, she was talking to Boris, although Boris wasn't really involved in the conversation. It was for my benefit. She was telling him at high volume about her friend who had just given birth and how they left her for hours in pain. It was clearly a pathetic attempt to upset me. She was trying to do it directly yesterday, but I put on my best, *'I'm not taking your shit on'* face, so today she thought she'd have another go at bringing me down. The more I learn about Jane, the more I think she must have some serious problems. The only way she can feel good about herself is to make others feel bad. I'm not sure I've ever met anyone as sad as her, she must be genuinely damaged. I'm not going to allow myself to get angry about it. That's what she wants. She wants others to feel as bad as her. I'm going to focus on the prospects I have, I've got college coming up, I've got a family I didn't have this time last year. If I take an honest stock take of my life, it's actually pretty good. If I was to focus on the negative, I'd have to be stupid.

One week from now, I'm due to be a father, I'm going to have all the responsibility on me that I've placed on my own father. All the trips, the holidays, the sports that I've been into over the years, my parents have had to take a certain amount of responsibility. I've got to focus on that.

I can feel in my bones a couple of really good things coming up. I'm not sure, but I just feel like I'm the crest of something really good. This is what I'll be thinking about as I go to sleep tonight. Not how much of a twat Jane is.

Friday September 7th 2012

No sign of the baby; Alison is getting really fed up now.

Saturday September 8th 2012

Alison sent me to my mum's today. She wanted some time on her own with her own mum. I was glad to get out the house, it's hard work looking after someone who can't move very much.

Mum and Dad took me for lunch. They're both over-excited about this coming week. All I can think about is how much it could be a terrifying experience, which is harder to deal with when you've got two excitable people who just aren't focusing on that side of things.

Sunday September 9th 2012

No sign of the baby or of any movement. Every sign of a stressed expectant mother and father.

Monday September 10th 2012

No movement.

Jane was slamming about the kitchen today. I've spoken to HR about the dates I'll be off and they're OK with me going when I need to and taking two weeks off after that. Jane is not so happy about it because 'she needs to plan'. Although what she's really unhappy about is that I won't be there to pick up on all the work that Boris doesn't do. She's ridiculous.

Tuesday September 11th 2012

*** Due Date ***

Nothing. No baby at all.

I went to work as usual. I've had my phone on the loudest possible setting for the last month and even with regular trips to the outside bins and numerous phone calls to check it's working, the news just isn't there for Alison to ring me with.

Half of me wants it to come so I don't have to be at work, the other half wishes my phone would break so her mum has to go with her and deal with the nasty stuff. I know I shouldn't think like that, but I can't help it. I'm scared that Jane wasn't lying about her 'friend'. The logical side of me knows it's very unlikely that she has any friends at all and I already know she's a complete arse, but it doesn't stop the negative part of my thinking grabbing on to what she said and using it to beat myself with.

Alison had her appointment with the midwife. She just came round and asked some questions, and then did a 'sweep' which is not as nice as it sounds. She basically puts her hand inside and checks where things are. The results are, no more movement, the baby is still engaged, but there is no dilation. We just wait now.

Monday September 17th 2012

The last week has just been an endless round of waiting. There is nothing to report other than a really uncomfortable Alison and a really tired me.

The midwife is coming round tomorrow, so hopefully there'll be something she can do something to help Mother Nature along.

Tuesday September 18th 2012

Another sweep. Still no dilation. She's booked us in for inducement on Monday. I asked if that was a bit later than the ten days the last midwife told us they'd allow us to go over, but apparently they're all booked on Friday and the weekend isn't the best time as they don't have as many staff on.

You'd think if they have a time frame they'd stick to it and not change it because they can't staff as much. I doubt the risk is any lower at a weekend. I'm trying not to get angry with the NHS. It's only me that'll get harmed.

Saturday September 22nd 2012

I got a film for us to watch today, I wanted to try and take both our minds off Monday. The wait is now really doing both our heads in. We got an Indian, too, Alison has been drinking all sorts of weird tea after reading on the Internet that it'll bring on the birth. There's so many old wives tales about what will bring the birth forward and all of them are bollocks.

Alison was crying throughout the film, even at the funny stuff, she is uber-emotional. Me? I held my eyes wide open to make sure I couldn't be accused of crying when the dog died in *Marley And Me*.

Sunday September 23rd 2012

23.00 p.m.

I think the waters have broken. Alison says she is unsure.

23.10 p.m.

Just Googled. Most people say we'll be ever so sure if they have broken. Alison is ringing the Ward anyway.

23.25 p.m.

The Ward have said we need to come and see them at nine in the morning. Alison is getting some pain, but not much. It's starting, though. I can't believe nine months has passed, it's flown by.

I'm going to become a father tomorrow.

To Be Continued ...

BRIDE AND GLOOM

ABOUT THE AUTHOR

Pete is 33 and lives with his wife, Lucie; daughter, Lilly; and their pet sofa, Jeff. He's been writing for just under three years and they've been pretty eventful; well, more eventful than he thought sitting on Jeff, typing, would be, anyway.

First published in the *Radgepacket* anthology with a story he'd written during month five of his new hobby, Pete's now featured in a total of ten different anthologies and has been amongst some very fine company. (Although he was the best in all of them, he knows that because both his mum and Jeff told him and they're both honest-to-God Christians ... possibly.)

Author of comedy e-books *The Village Idiot Reviews*, *The Office Idiot Reviews*, *The Idiot Government Reviews* and *More Village Idiot Reviews*, Pete has seen these books sell more than he ever thought they would, and he's hooked. *Dating in the Dark* is Pete's first self-published novel. His traditionally published novel, *So Low, So High*, was published by Caffeine Nights in June 2013.

Contact Pete:

Facebook:
https://www.facebook.com/Pete.Sortwell.Author

Twitter: @petesortwell

email: petesortwell@googlemail.com

OTHER TITLES

THE DIARY OF A HAPLESS FATHER

Not only is Graham Peterson unlucky in his choice of careers, he's also been terrible with women throughout his adult life. That changed when he met Alison, but within a month of meeting, he got the news that he was about to become a father for the first time.

The Diary of a Hapless Father charts those first three terrifying months of parenthood. With all the angst and fear of a new father, Graham needs to pull his socks up if he's going to become the father he always dreamed he would be.

With all the pitfalls and worries of a new father charted, this book is for all those who have been through early parenthood or just want to know how a man deals with all those things internally.

SO LOW, SO HIGH

Most people generally don't drink white cider for breakfast, don't use the aisle of Tesco as a toilet and don't steal from their family and friends. Simon Brewster does though. He's a doomed man. Living life day to day, stealing Edam balls and legs of lamb, ducking and diving his way from petty theft to dealer and back again. If he doesn't change his ways, he'll never see middle age, let alone old age.

He's seen his parents on their knees, crying, begging him to stop; he's been arrested by his former best mate; he's been hospitalised, all as a result of drugs and alcohol. It's just not enough to make him stop.

Simon lies to everyone, including himself. The truth is, he has no more idea why he does the things he does than you do. What he needs is a way out. But if such a thing exists, Simon hasn't had much luck finding it. He's powerless and his life is unmanageable to the point of insanity.

This is the story of Simon Brewster's last year using class A drugs. Join him as he crashes his way through police cells, courtrooms and display cabinets. One way or another, Simon will stop using drugs. But can the people that love him help him overcome his addictions before his addictions destroy him?

Available from Caffeine Nights Publishing.

THE VILLAGE IDIOT REVIEWS

Join Brian as he tries to woo the girl that works in the local shop; will passing out face down in super glue while trying to make her a gift hinder his chances of getting her to go out with him?

Will Father Frederick, an alcoholic vicar who has a slight issue with stalking, be able to win back the heart of a woman he loved a long time ago?

And will Ethel, who thinks that throwing hard rice instead of confetti in a bridegroom's face is an acceptable form of sport, be able to catch one of these two losers in love with her trick as they step out of the church on the happy day?

Written entirely in the form of product reviews, we guarantee you've never read a book quite like this before. Hilarious and wholly original, *The Village Idiot Reviews* pokes gentle fun at the more obscure corners of your favourite e-commerce sites – and introduces the most bonkers set of countryside dwellers since The Vicar of Dibley.

THE OFFICE IDIOT REVIEWS

There are all sorts of idiots we have to work with every day. Every office has them. Fortunately for most of us idiots in the work place are few and far between. However, Hogsbottom Plugs, 'the home of bath plugs' has a higher concentration than other workplaces, from the MD down to the cleaner, they're all Idiots.

Read the trials and tribulations of this idiotic workforce as they explain their recent life events through reviews of things they've bought. There's Donald, who try as hard as he does, simply cannot get the office junior to notice him, let alone drink some of his special, sleeping tablet-laced tea. Learn how Jeff gets his own back on the people who mock him by re-enacting a video he saw on YouTube involving seagulls, and watch in horror as the over-worked cleaner tries to solve the mystery of who is making his job of cleaning the toilets worse than a job cleaning toilets is already.

If you've ever worked in an office, then this is the book for you. You'll recognise the office sex pest, the liar and the moaning admin worker who's been there longer than the chairs. Written in the form of product reviews, *The Office Idiot Reviews* is the second in the series of 'Idiot Review' books from Pete Sortwell.

THE IDIOT GOVERNMENT REVIEWS

We've all seen the news over the last few years, watching in wonder and disbelief at the situations the people entrusted to run the country get themselves into and then proceed to lie their way out of. Just imagine, and this won't be hard, that they were so stupid that they wrote reviews of the items that got them into or out of their latest bit of trouble and posted them online.

Ted Williebond is angry, not only at having to settle for running the opposition, but also for the bullying he had to endure at school by Cameron Davies and Gary Osburn, who now run the Government and don't mind pointing that out to Ted every time they see him. Join Ted as he foolishly leaves reviews of such items as Silly String, vodka and thick curtains as he tries his hardest to bring down the coalition.

On the other side of the fence we've got Daniel Dangly, a foolhardy old school politician from Southamptonshire who, try as he might, cannot outrun the press, who seem to stalk him for easy stories; and Elouise Munch, a career girl more concerned about who's defaced her designer handbag than the people in her constituency.

Running the show though isn't Cameron Davies or Ted Williebond; in fact it is Betty Rivers, the CEO of Information Inc.

THE COMPLETE IDIOT REVIEWS

The first three 'Idiot' reviews books are now available from Amazon in e-book format as a handy box set.

MORE VILLAGE IDIOT REVIEWS

It's been a year since their last outing. Brian, Ethel and Father Frederick are back with more village idiocy.

Frederick has injured his nipples in a vicious moped accident whilst on his honeymoon and no longer feels like a man. He's taken up the drink again and is making people's lives a misery with his antics again. He can't work out why strange men keep following him while he's out drink-driving, though.

Brian's concentrating on getting through married life while trying to find a hobby that doesn't hurt. His cousin Jeff (from *The Office Idiot Reviews*) has moved in for the summer and is on hand to help Brian with his assertiveness when he is bullied by the local biker, Jock.

Ethel has discovered that it was Denny who made her shopping trolley explode last year and with Denny now an adult and living outside the safety of the children's home, it won't be long before she exacts the revenge she's been after.

Meanwhile a battle for power is taking place at the manor house. Lord Monty, who ordered his title from the Internet, is in a battle of wills with his gamekeeper, Chopper. It's a never ending struggle which, time after time, leaves Monty either out of pocket, in pain or soaking wet.

Written entirely in the form of product reviews, we guarantee you've never read a book quite like this before. (Unless you read the first one.) Hilarious and wholly original, *More Village Idiot Reviews* introduces the most bonkers set of countryside dwellers you've ever had the pleasure of meeting.

DATING IN THE DARK: SOMETIMES LOVE JUST PRETENDS TO BE BLIND

Jason is single and has been for all of his 32 years. It's depressing. But not as depressing as being told by his mother that he looks like Humpty Dumpty – after the accident. With a face that not even his own mother can love, it's hardly surprising that he'll try anything to get a woman to go out with him, even if it's only for a single date.

With little interest in anything other than his quest for a woman and a nice bit of cod and chips, Jason needs to think outside the box if he's going to find someone who'll give him a chance. Along with Barry – his best mate – Jason comes up with the only thing he thinks will work: dating a blind woman.

However, to do that, he needs to pretend he's blind himself, which is a lot harder than you might think ... especially when guide dogs are so hard to come by. Eventually Jason's efforts pay off and he meets Emma, a pretty professional with a host of friends. When he takes her out, they instantly hit it off. But will Jason be able to fool both Emma and her best friend Jerry into thinking he's blind? With everything to play for, Jason faces the biggest challenge of his life, and nobody – especially not him – can see how it'll all turn out.

BRIDE AND GLOOM: SOMETIMES LOVE IS BETTER OFF BLIND

In the first book of the 'Sometimes love ...' series, 'Dating in the Dark: sometimes love just pretends to be blind', Jason Harding thought he'd committed the ultimate betrayal. No, not cheating; he pretended to be, you guessed it, blind. For Emma, the woman he was stupid enough to think he was fooling, it wasn't anything like a betrayal. It was both sweet and sad at the same time and, as people in relationships have a tendency to do (if they don't split up because of one party's wild lies), Emma and Jason decide to get married.

Just how Jason manages to deal with the huge life change that is marriage is what this book is about. From getting his specially made suit tailored to his short height, to trying to keep a lid on his best man's plans for a wild weekend in Liverpool, he is going to struggle to make to through to the wedding without having a full nervous breakdown. His second best friend, Boris, also returns in this book, although he has lost his taxi, his wife and his ability to seem sober even when he's drunk six litres of vodka.

Jason is foolish enough to add Neil, Emma's wayward cousin, and Terry, the owner of Jason's favourite fish and chip shop, to his list of groomsmen. This is the fairly tragic band of men that are to ensure Jason makes it to the church on time, in possession of both his of his eyebrows and, of course, the rings ...

Printed in Great Britain
by Amazon.co.uk, Ltd.,
Marston Gate.